AF225860

ARE WE ALL F*CKED?

CAN WE THRIVE IN LIFE?
CAN WE BE HAPPY IN RELATIONSHIPS?

ELDIN HASA

Have an inward experience and a new you will emerge.

Are we all F*cked?

Dedicated to my Wife

Have an inward experience and a new you will emerge.

Contents:

Are We All F*CKED?
Dedication
Intro   **1**
ABOUT THE AUTHOR   **4**
Chapter 1- Emotional Fitness   **10**
Chapter 2 -You   **24**
Chapter 3 - Emotional muscles   **31**
Chapter 4 - Who am I?   **38**
Chapter 5 - The Universe   **49**
Chapter 6 - Conduit of Universal Consciousness **61**
Chapter 7- I AM   **72**
Chapter 8 - Self-Love   **80**
Chapter 9- Removing negative habits   **87**
Chapter 10 - Mental Health   **95**
Chapter 11- TRANSFORMATION   **101**
Chapter 12 - Love   **111**
Chapter 13 - Ideal Partner   **119**
Chapter 14 - Can we be Happy in Relationships?   **125**
Chapter 15 - Overcoming Difficulties in a Relationship **135**
Chapter 16 - Magical Relationship   **142**
Chapter 17 - Relationship With Children **157**
Chapter- 18 - MEDITATION   **172**
Chapter 19 - Positive habits   **182**
Support resources   **196**
Copyright

Have an inward experience and a new you will emerge.

Intro

Are we all fucked?

You would probably get different answers if you ask the same question to several people. It depends on who you ask and depending on their perception and their level of awareness or awakening. If they have ever experienced the infinite possibilities of who they indeed are as a human being.

If you ask Laszlo, who has focussed most of his life on the lack and limitations, you will get resounding yes. He has never experienced thriving in life and has focused on blaming the government, society, boss, economy, spouse, everything, and everyone else for his shortcomings. He lived most of his lives below his true potential, and never experienced how amazing he truly is, deep at his core. Laszlo has never done any deep internal work, meditated, or practiced any other positive personal development rituals. He might have tried a couple of things, meditated once for ten minutes, and concluded that he hates this personal development fluffy stuff. Laszlo told me several times that he wants other people to change so he could be happy. He believed that other people's actions are somehow responsible for how he feels and that if they'd only changed and behaved differently, he would have a good relationship, and feel better. Laszlo spent most of his time on reading negative information, following news propaganda and fear mongers, negative videos, violent video games, negative social media.

(Laszlo-A fictional name used for confidentiality reasons).

He was experiencing a lot of emotional pain and trauma. Doing a lot of addictive rituals, which could be detrimental to his mental and physical health. Laszlo was full of self-doubt and self-limiting beliefs in his life. Having never been courageous to live from his heart and soul fully, he would try to present facts and figures, ideas, and stories about the doom and gloom and share his life experiences from subjective self-limiting beliefs. Laszlo would do anything and say anything to protect his limited negative paradigm and say that we are all fucked.

If you ask the same question to Aniko, who is truly thriving in her life and always has been, the answer would be no. She has been doing positive daily rituals to connect deeply in her heart and soul and to who she truly is. She practices positive daily habits and rituals and chooses to only feed her mind with positive content that elevates and inspires her. Aniko is always in the flow and creating everything effortlessly, whatever the economy is doing, and has the most amazing deep, meaningful relationships at home with her family, loved ones, and with her friends. She is experiencing an abundance of health, love, money, and profound happiness and fulfilment in her life. She never blamed anything or anyone and always knew that she is responsible for herself and her life.
 Aniko is a person who does a lot of philanthropy and is contributing positively to humanity, giving from her heart effortlessly. Aniko will tell you that this is the best time to be alive. That 2019 it's the best year to create and contribute; this is the time with unlimited possibilities. The time to heal ourselves, contribute positively to humanity and help improve the planet.
And as we are healing ourselves from within and removing blockages and self-limiting beliefs and

releasing past stories, pains, and traumas, through having an experience of who we indeed are, we are creating a positive ripple effect on everyone around us and paying it forward. As a result, we are healing the planet and changing the world.

We are more creative and produce more when we do deep internal work and focus on healing ourselves. As we concentrate on releasing old stories, old self-limiting beliefs, past traumas, and experience who and what we indeed are, we begin to feel infinite deep self-love, self-confidence, and experience unlimited possibilities. Suddenly we begin to experience countless positive coincidences, serendipities, and synchronicities in our lives.

(Aniko- A fictional name used for confidentiality reasons).

ABOUT THE AUTHOR

This book is about real-life events. It's a book about his journey, insights, and experiences of many of his coaching clients. Feeling incomplete as a human being, having gone through several major relationship traumas, and gone through financial ruin, he sets out on the search for the wisdom to live a happy, healthy, and more fulfilling life. Throughout his travels around the world, he has studied for over 25 years with countless mentors, gurus, monks, and teachers; Eldin discovers a pearl of powerful wisdom that shapes his reality, helps him access his higher self, and achieve magnificent transformation. The lessons Eldin learns through his extraordinary adventure will inspire you to want to create wonderful changes in your life as well. These are the same lessons used to transform me, and the lives of many of my coaching clients for over ten years. I experienced traumas, setbacks on the journey throughout my life. Yet, each stumbling block has eventually presented as a stepping stone and has brought me closer to my heart's truth and the best version of who I truly am and always was. Some years ago, I was working as a successful property investor and developer, chasing financial success and all the material objects that went along with it, thinking that this was the way to lasting happiness and fulfilment. But as I work harder and achieved more financial success, I realised that nothing ever really changed, I was still unhappy, and many of my important relationships suffered. No matter how many material possessions I gathered, the man I saw in the mirror every morning was the same miserable person, looking for the next fix. I wasn't any happier and didn't feel any better. The more I reflected on the state of my life; I realised I was living in a very restrictive way of my true human potential and just going with the motions reacting to life. I became aware of emptiness within my heart and began to observe many unhealthy behaviours and habits. I started paying attention to its silent whispers, which instructed me to leave my chosen profession and start some serious soul-searching. I started to think about why I was here on this tiny planet and what my special mission was. I wondered why I was so unhappy and unfulfilled and what significant changes needed to be made to feel more fulfilled.

I evaluated my core beliefs, assumptions, values, rituals, and filters through which I saw myself and the world, and I committed myself to eradicate the less than healthy ones.

During the period of intense transformation, I read countless books on self-help, personal leadership, philosophy, and spirituality. I took personal-development courses, studied psychology, Cognitive Behavioural Therapy (CBT), and Positive Psychology Resilience Skills, Emotional Fitness, Relationships, Neuroscience, Quantum Physics, traveled around the world to study with gurus, monks, and spiritual teachers for many years. After years of countless trials (using myself as a human guineapig), I changed my diet, my thinking, my behaviours, my rituals, my patterns, and eventually, the person I evolved into was someone more authentic, harmonious, fulfilled and wiser than the person I once was. I am still a work in progress on this journey of self-discovery, and I'm by no means a finished article. Having worked as a therapist and coach for over ten years, I am very passionate about helping people and inspiring them to want to become the best versions of themselves. While I'm writing this book, I am moving through yet another period of enormous personal growth and personal transformation and reassessing my fundamental values along with the way I view the world. As I wake up at 4 am every day and start to have greater clarity, more certainty I began to experience new blessings in every area of my life; to me, that's what the unfolding of magic and miracle of life is all about. I hope that the ideas, insights, and wisdom I share in this book touches you deeply and propels you into taking massive action to improve your own life, and your relationships so you too can feel profoundly happy and fulfilled.

◆ ◆ ◆

How to read this book?
Read one chapter and meditate on it; try to have an inward experience. And don't try to understand it intellectually. I suggested that within 24 hours of completing this book, you share ideas and the wisdom you've learned with someone you care about. Doing this will clarify your understanding and assist you in integrating the lessons into your own life. I also hope that you have fun living the knowledge of this book, bringing the childlike sense of wonder and passion to what you discover on the pages that follow is one of the best ways to grow into the person I know you're meant to be. Thank you for giving me the privilege of sharing this work with you. I wish for you a life abundant with love, joy, peace, magic, relationship bliss, profound happiness, and fulfilment, and I hope that you do your part in paying it forward and help in creating a better world.

◆ ◆ ◆

Adventures of Eldin: Eldin is a Success Coach, Entrepreneur, Investor, Leader, Relationship Coach, Father, Husband, Motivational Speaker, Author and an

accredited Master Practitioner of Neuro-linguistic
Programming (NLP) Master Coach in London. Certified
in Cognitive Behavioural Therapy (CBT) and Positive
Psychology Resilience and Relationships Skills.
Relationship Bliss?
It is all about relationships, a relationship with oneself,
with others, and what everyone is striving for is to
experience profound happiness, fulfilment, and authentic
relationship bliss.

I specialise in; Relationship Coaching, Emotional
Fitness, Removal of Traumas, and Leadership Coaching.
Functional coaching produces profound transformational
results in only a handful of sessions. I focus on the root
cause and not the symptoms.

◆ ◆ ◆

10 + years experience
He has worked with many clients from all walks of life
as well as high-performance clients including, lawyers,
finance professionals, athletes, CEOs, entrepreneurs,
psychiatrists, ex-military, influencers, and coaches.
Eldin is very proud of the success achieved after
working with the number of suicide survivors.
 He often goes to public schools in London and holds
free motivational talks to disadvantaged children sharing
some of his positive wisdom in the hope that he could
help influence at least one person positively and
potentially save a life or future imprisonment. Eldin is
experienced in personal development, and peak
performance having traveled the world and studied with
some of the best mentors, teachers and gurus for over 25
years and continuously working on himself, having
received coaching and mentoring on various subjects, in
multiple areas of life including psychology, meaningful
relationships, love, dating, feminine and masculine
energies, entrepreneurship, sales, neuroscience, quantum

physics, various types of meditation including mindfulness and Kundalini Sahaja yoga meditation, black belt in number of martial art disciplines and practitioner of MMA. Eldin qualified as a personal fitness trainer in his late teens and worked teaching about health, fitness, and nutrition for some years. This is where he started to develop his love for helping people, listening skills, Eldin is happily married to Nadia, a very successful financial regulation lawyer in the Magic Circle in the City of London. They've been in a deep, meaningful relationship for six years, full of unconditional love, joy, happiness, and profound fulfilment. Been happily married for over two years, and look forward to growing old and happy together. Eldin met Nadia six years ago at the gym in London. It was a love at first sight. He noticed her long chestnut brown hair, her big brown eyes, and her warm smile with a hint of shyness, and her lips were like a beautiful rose. Nadia is Eldin's best friend, love of his life, and he makes sure to tell her each day how grateful he is to have her in his life. He thanks her several times each day for "being so amazing." Note: "Bing amazing," not doing or having as most of us are conditioned to focus on. Most of us only express our gratitude to another when they have done something for us or have given us something. One of the pearls of wisdom learned from one of his Gurus is that we should express gratitude to another just for being alive. Eldin & Nadia hit it off on the very first date six years ago. They were very much in love and very affectionate form the first encounter. Often they talk about how grateful they are for being as affectionate now, if not even more as on the first date, and that they are so thankful to be more so in love each day. They've cultivated a deep, meaningful relationship, devoted, respectful, understanding, compassionate, kind, supportive, and full of profound love and admiration for each other. Their goal is to introduce to the world; the insights, experiences, and techniques on how to have the same type of relationship full of deep love for oneself and others, and enjoy pure joy in life, and experience the true relationship bliss.

 Eldin wasn't born with any special powers or talents, and he didn't have a rich uncle who left him a fortune to start him off on his business journey, he is a regular guy with a deep passion for learning, hardworking and passion for helping people.

◆ ◆ ◆

GURU OF LOVE AND RESILIENCE

Eldin truly understands human suffering, love, relationships and is very compassionate. Having overcome significant relationship traumas, being on the receiving end of domestic violence, breakup, adultery, burnout, breakdown, illness in the family, grief, financial crises, addiction, lawsuit, to name a few. Whatever your current situation - you too can turn your life around with Eldin's guidance.

Chapter 1- EMOTIONAL FITNESS

I had a vision of one indeed United World where all the people have profoundly open their hearts, and confidently feel vulnerable, and are living in peace and harmony, in love, compassion, and kindness. A world of solidarity and equality, everyone is communicating and contributing from a place of compassion, love, and respect where neighbours are interacting on a deep level, where everyone is cooperating and collaborating freely, unconditionally, and without wanting anything in return. A world where everyone is living from a place of creativity and confidence, feeling inspired and profoundly happy and fulfilled. Where all the people are thriving and not just surviving, a world where there is no more suffering, hunger, poverty, inequality, or wars. Everyone is connected deeply in their hearts and souls and feels that we are truly one. Everyone is living in prosperity and abundance of health, love, happiness, fulfilment, and money. I can feel that in 2020 something big is coming, in the shape of selflessness, unity, solidarity and love. I believe the best part of humanity and who we indeed are is unconditional love, selflessness, patience, compassion, and kindness. The part of humanity that wants to protect the innocent and defend the vulnerable, that's the best of humanity. Every human being wants to avoid pain and suffering, to feel loved, to feel truly happy and fulfilled. A world where news and newspapers only talk about inspiring, uplifting, positive stories, sharing insights on how to love oneself deeply, and how to truly love others. A world where people not only respect and love each other but also animals, plants, environment, nature, and all of creation.

My mission with this book is to spread love and positivity, and help people realise how great they are, and that all the power, love, confidence, creativity and abundance resides inside of them, and with unlimited possibilities. In this book, I will share inspiring personal experiences with many tools, techniques, and strategies on how you can help yourself to realise how amazing you are, just for existing in this body. The goal is to help elevate the human consciousness, and to help people live more from their heart, and less from their head. To live less in fear, have more confidence, creativity, compassion, inspiration, self-love, and more self-worth. To have more emotional resilience and develop high emotional fitness.
The mission is to help children, the young generation, and millennials feel more self-love, self-worth, and self-confidence. So together, we can heal our pain and help improve the planet. The mission is peace & love for all the people around the world, and all of creation.

When my coaching clients come to see me, they often want to know how to do something. Clients ask me; how to improve in certain areas of their life, how to improve their relationship, how to overcome certain challenges, how to meditate, how to overcome certain traumas, suffering, how to remove self-limiting beliefs, how to stop self-harm, how to overcome some addictions. Everyone seems to be focusing predominantly on 'How To' and desiring a quick fix, and they are eager to learn the next strategy in how to get this, that or the other. I used to focus on the same, followed some of the best' How To' step by step strategies to achieve a certain outcome in life, business, and achieved (what society calls) success, but I was feeling unhappy and unfulfilled. I've seen countless clients and personal friends, millionaires, and billionaires grow their business, grow their bank account, increasing the number of material objects exponentially, but still deep inside feel extremely unhappy and unfulfilled. A lot of my clients say, "If a person thinks that money will bring them happiness, they probably don't have any." Many of my clients clearly know how to do, and they have access to countless strategies and techniques on how to achieve something by following a number of practical steps. There are countless books written on 'How To'..... Seven steps to a perfect beach body. Twelve steps to making a million. Ten steps to making the law of attraction work for you. How to improve your business, income, body, anything. You name it; there are several books and strategies out there that could help you achieve your external results. And you will often grow your bank account, your business, buy that dream house, dream car, get that perfect spouse, and when you get all of that, in the majority of cases, you will feel unhappy and unfulfilled. So you will go on looking externally for the next thing that you could do or have in order to feel the profound happiness and fulfilment. So each time you do or have the next thing, you realise more and more, that you are unhappy and unfulfilled, and then you feel the pain in your body, and this pain is often ignored and or brushed under the carpet, with detrimental addictive behaviours such as drugs, alcohol, gambling, food, sex, workaholism, self-abuse, and in some cases suicide. The suicide rate is at it's highest than ever before. You realise that this way of life is not sustainable, and it often leads to detrimental mental and physical health. The issues in significant relationships, financial crisis, and potentially loss of everything external, that we perceive as important in our life.

For those of you who might be thinking, yes, Eldin, I hear you; it's all good and well that you work with a lot of successful people. How can your book or your coaching help me pay my rent next month? Will it help me find a job, get out of debt, or make more money? Can it help me find an ideal partner, or fix my relationship with my girlfriend? Will it help me to stop arguing with my husband, and how do I improve my relationship with my children? I have worked for over ten years with people from all walks of life, children, teenagers, victims of sexual abuse, people who self-harm, suicide survivors, and homeless people. People are people with nuances of the same patterns of doing things externally to feel the desired emotions or avoid feeling some feelings. No matter who I work with; billionaire , homeless person, religious person or atheist, gay or straight, young or old, he, she or it, deep down on the inside, at their core, they are all the same and have variations of the same issues and feel the same pain. We realised that we have only focussed on Doing and Having and paid little emphasis on Being.
Being is the foundation for everything. It is where our deep emotions and feelings are situated and experienced.

BEING

I could say that there are two aspects of what makes us human beings:
- One is the societal human being; as seen by society, our physical body. Most of us focus only on this aspect.
- The other is our invisible internal human being, that is known, written about in countless texts for thousands of years. In the last hundred years, scientists have just begun to understand it, but confirmed that it certainly exists and that it's our source of everything, including the source of co-creation of everything in our physical

reality. More people have begun to focus on this aspect.

In my studies, and my own life, I've discovered that there is a way that we can cultivate profound happiness, self-love, and fulfilment, and also go after achieving a lot of external success at the same time. Having met a lot of successful people in my life, it is a rarity that they are profoundly happy and fulfilled. Often when you probe them, they'd tell you that they are very unhappy. I have also met a handful of people who have it all; a ton of money, abundance in every aspect, deep, meaningful relationships, profound self-love, and they are the happiest and most fulfilled people I have ever met. All of them have several attributes in common, which I will be sharing throughout this book, and all of them have mastered the art of emotional fitness, amongst other things.

I help clients with ; the why, and bring awareness inwardly, that at their core, they are already perfect, created in a perfect image by god/universe and that everything they have been looking for externally, already resides within them since birth. I help them remove certain impediments in order to see who they indeed are, and what they're capable of. I help my clients live more from their hearts, remain open, vulnerable and deeply connected, and less from the head.

I hear a lot of people talk about how they'd like to change the world and make an impact. A lot of them are very passionate, and trying to do something about it, but often in a way that is not sustainable, because they haven't improved or grown from within as human beings.

I could write an entire book about what is wrong with the world today; about geopolitical unrest, Brexit, poverty, hunger, global warming, corruption, racism, modern-day slavery, industrial animal farming, excessive fishing, and mass destruction of our planet. I could probably write thousands of books, but we all know what is going on out there, and I would be writing about the problems and stating the obvious.

Instead, I have written a book, focusing on solutions, and all the fantastic aspects of what makes us human beings. I believe that, the way to make the best and quickest positive impact on the world, which is also sustainable, is by making sure that you work on yourself daily and constantly. Do deep internal work through meditation and remove any impediments (pains, traumas) that are holding you back, from recognising how amazing you already are, who and what you truly are. And becoming aware that you already are the infinite love, infinite abundance and infinite possibilities. As you do this, and heal from within, you create a positive ripple effect on everyone around you and help heal the planet, and help improve the world. Imagine a world where millions of people commit for the next ninety days to work on themselves, starting today. They divert their entire energy, and focus on healing and unveiling the best version of themselves, and in the process heal the world. No need to fight and protest against something, use your entire energy to work on yourself and stand united in solidarity for peace, love, equality, and compassion. As Mother Teresa said: Don't invite me to fight and protest against something, if you invite me to stand with you for peace and love, I'll be there.

There is No way to Happiness! Happiness is the Way! First you need to learn and develop the feeling of gratitude and happiness on the inside. The expression is BE Happy, not DO happy or HAVE happy. You cannot Go and Do happy.

If you don't develop profound happiness from within, NOTHING you DO or HAVE will ever make you happy or fulfilled. Everything we do is because of the feelings we desire to feel. We might be doing different things. We might be focusing on different types of achievements, have different goals, but ultimately we are all doing those things to arrive to the feelings.

What if there is a way to feel these feelings all the time? What if there is a way to intensify these feelings everyday? What if you could do something positive everyday to feel the feelings you desire? Feeling of profound and sustainable happiness and fulfilment. Feeling of deep inner peace, bliss, joy, profound self-love and self-confidence.

Deep down inside I know I'm going to be okay! Have you ever said this or heard someone say it?
What if deep down inside is the place that we don't only visit when we have a problem, when we have a crisis in a relationship, love, romance, business, finance, emotional, mental and physical health? What if, deep down inside is the place you could visit every day? What if deep down inside is the place you could do everything from all the time? What if we could do daily positive rituals that bring us connected deeper and deeper to the deep down inside? The deep down inside where infinite love, infinite intelligence, and infinite abundance resides.
What if deep down inside is the direct vibrational energetic frequency to the universal consciousness, to the divine guidance, to the unlimited possibilities? It is the feeling of joy, love, creativity, peace, bliss,

abundance, confidence, inspiration, and happiness that we are all seeking.
Resulting in doing numerous activities to bring us closer, and to deepen the experience of those feelings. Some of the things we do, could be good for us, for our physical and mental health, but a lot of things we do could be detrimental to both our mental and physical health. And most importantly these negative activities and rituals we do, take us further away from those desired feelings of deep joy, bliss, confidence, love and abundance, and they are not sustainable.

Your daily habits and rituals have a direct impact on how you feel and success in every area of your life.
If you feed your mind with negative fear promoting news and negative conversations all day from the moment you wake up, you will undoubtedly be miserable and unfulfilled. And not to mention the energy required to feel so negative all day.
If you desire a good quality of life, give your mind positive and healthy diet and not just your body.

A lot of people do so many trivial activities each day, because they are trying to run away from the negative feelings. Past trauma that manifests as physical pain, the intensity fluctuates, depending on what activity they are doing.
We go on our phone, connect to social media, Facebook, Instagram, scroll aimlessly for hours each day, and often compare our lives and ourselves with others and their photoshopped perfect pictures and this creates further pain. The cycle continues, and the pain grows in intensity. We watch several hours a day of our favourite shows, download the entire show, all six seasons on our phones so we can watch on the train/tube on our commute to a job that we probably hate. We subject ourselves to many other addictive behaviours, such as

consumption of large quantities of alcohol, drugs, food, sex, and or other addictions that could be detrimental to our mental and physical health. We download so many apps on our phones, and get addicted to instant gratification.

You're hungry push a button and food arrives. Push a button and cab comes, swipe right/or was it left (not sure, never used it) and date arrives. You feel sad, message ten of your friends; 'hey', and most reply almost instantly. I've been told it's rude to read messages, and not to reply immediately. Anything can be delivered fast: food, flowers, furniture, clean laundry, instant answers on Google, groceries, even a date.

You have a potential date available almost instantly through one of the dating apps, right at your fingertips, waiting for you to filter them by location, sexuality, religion, hobbies, and how desperate they are for a partner. No need for hard work or much effort.

Such demand for instantaneous gratification has repercussions beyond internet usage and purchasing habits; a society that experiences fewer and fewer waits in its daily habits will slowly have less and less patience. In specific fields, a lack of patience is fine. Still, when raising children, teaching others, or climbing the professional ladder, there is no way around slow, sometimes painful periods of growth.

There is no app available to instantly get deep, meaningful relationships, mental and physical health, career success, thriving business, financial success, joy, profound happiness, fulfilment, self-love, and self-confidence.

People today need to get a better grasp on what it takes to succeed. There is nothing wrong with starting at the bottom; everyone was a beginner at some point. All super successful people have a beginner's mentality and child-like sense of curiosity, and always willing to learn something new, even after having all the money in the world, and all the success.

Allowing yourself to feel and experience growth and deep expansion should be your primary focus. Do not continue to convince yourself that you're a failure or that others have it easier than you. Your chosen path of entitlement has not worked. Now choose another way. You can accomplish anything you want. But no one can achieve it for you.

Practice positive rituals daily and consistently.

Take better care of your health. Choose a healthy diet, exercise.

Be proactive in every aspect of your life. Build your life. Make a high-quality effort. Give it time. Let the compound effect of daily positive actions show long terms results. Lose your expectation of instant gratification, and you will succeed.

We do so many things because we want people to like us; we crave their validation, and their approval. We are so worried about what other people think of us, so we live in fear to be our true selves, to be our authentic selves, and express our true potential just to fit in.

We create labels for those feelings which act as a guide/ compass for what we do or not do. We say things like; this is my personality, it's my character, it's who I am, these are my values and my beliefs, it is in my culture, I can't change. No one can change.

Whatever we call them or label then, they come from deep down inside in the form of feelings, and intuitively we know, that we are guided to act from these feelings. These feelings are guiding us to do the right thing or say the right things at that moment.

How many times have we had the feeling from this deep down inside, that we shouldn't have done something or said something, that backfired, and caused detriment to us and others? And we said to ourselves, I should have listened. I had a feeling, not to do or say. Raise your arm if you have experienced this. My arm has risen very high, I can assure you. It's the same place, deep down inside, that we all know so well. It's always available to us, to guide us, protect us, keep us safe, give us unconditional love, provide us with infinite intelligence, infinite creativity, and infinite abundance.

We've gone the wrong way about it, to get to these feelings that reside in all of us.
What if we have been told that, in order to get to all of those internal feelings of infinite love, abundance, joy, creativity, and happiness, we need to go and get something externally first?
We need to do something externally or get something externally to experience those feelings. But the more we buy into the myth that something, or someone external of us, is required as an intermediary, for us to feel the feelings, which reside inside of us, the further away we separate ourselves from experiencing those feelings. And it becomes a never-ending cycle, where we feel the need to do more or get more on the outside, to experience the feelings on the inside. We live in the constant illusion that something or someone is the source of our happiness, abundance, love, creativity, inspiration, joy, and bliss.

There are two fundamental feelings (basic human needs) that we are internally guided to do everything from:
1. Feeling of Love & Connection; to feel that we are loved, lovable, loving, accepted, appreciated, valued, understood, seen, noticed, acknowledged, feeling that we are good enough.
2. Fear of rejection, not loved, not valued, not appreciated, not accepted, not understood, fear that we are not good enough.

Most of us struggle with difficult emotions and moods because we were never taught much about our emotions, either how they work or how to work with them. They never taught us in school about emotions or emotional fitness. Our parents and family did the best they could with the knowledge they had. As a result, most of us feel bad for having them and try to make them go away as fast as possible. But, when we try to eliminate or escape from painful emotions, we only train our minds to be more reactive to them. Instead of continually trying to fix or eradicate difficult emotions, what if we learned how to work with them? What if we could learn how to stop fighting our emotions and live alongside them? In short, what if we could build a better relationship with our emotions?

I believe the key to building a better relationship with our emotions and creating a healthier, more balanced emotional life is the regular practice of Emotional Fitness.

Building emotional fitness is vital.

Just understanding emotions is like going to a presentation, and a trainer is talking about how the treadmill works for an hour, you understand it and go home and do nothing. You have to get on the treadmill for an hour every day, for 90 days, six months, or one year to get the benefits.

There is no point in understanding emotions; you have to exercise your emotions every day. You have to build your emotional fitness every day.

There is a big difference between emotional intelligence (knowing) and emotional fitness. A lot of unfit people know a lot about the gym but never go or do any practice.

Everyone seems to be focusing only on mindset. You have to first focus on Soul-set and Heart-set to be in harmony; otherwise, you will feel out of balance.

Have an inward experience and a new you will emerge.

If you always focus on improving your body (appearance) mindset, (thinking) and never on your heart (emotions), and soul (spirituality), you will feel out of balance, and probably unhappy and unfulfilled.

Emotional fitness is a simple idea that our emotions need regular exercise, and training just as much as our bodies do, to stay healthy and fit. Emotional fitness is the idea that to lead healthy, happy emotional lives, we need consistent habits and exercise that support our mental health and wellbeing. Just like physical health depends on a foundation of good diet and exercise habits, our emotional health depends on a foundation of positive rituals and exercises.

Most people have an aversion to talking about or showing their feelings. As a result, they become distanced from their feelings, which makes it hard for them even to recognise how they feel at any given moment. And when adults do label their feelings, they often do it indirectly: Rather than saying, "I felt sad," someone might say, "I had a lump in my throat," or, "My eyes got watery." Or instead of saying, "I am nervous," someone might be more inclined to say, "I have butterflies in my stomach." Spend a few minutes every day, acknowledging your emotional state. Label your feelings and consider how those emotions are likely to affect your decisions. Whether you're feeling sad about something in your personal life, or worried about something going on at school, or the office, your emotions will spill over into other areas of your life if you aren't aware of them.

Activity

Before you continue reading, pause for a moment, close your eyes, take a few deep breaths, and focus internally on how you feel. Become aware of any feelings you may be feeling in your body. Now without thinking, write below any feelings that you might be feeling. Describe them in detail. Where in your body do you feel them? Do they feel hot or cold? Do they feel constricting or expanding? Are they familiar or unfamiliar feelings? The task is to experience them fully and profoundly. Sit with your emotions, for 30 minutes, without distraction, and experience them. Create space for anything that comes up, and it's okay if you cry or feel sad. It's how you release trapped emotions that have probably been there for years.

It is time to face your emotions and courageously take your full power back.

Chapter 2 -YOU

"Your relationship with yourself sets the tone for every other relationship you have."

If you hear the saying; You need to get out of your way. When you hear that, what does this mean to you? What are you experiencing when you hear this saying? What I am experiencing is; when I connect deeper to my heart and do more from deep down inside, or do less, I connect even more in-depth, and the desired emotions get intensified exponentially. It's a permanent place that resides in all of us, and it is who we indeed are. I am experiencing that, when I stop thinking and feel more from my heart, things miraculously start to manifest in my life. Beautiful coincidences, synchronicities, and serendipities start happening all around me. Problems start miraculously dissolving as if they were never there in the first place. The deeper I connect to the source of who I truly am, of who we all are, the deeper I feel the desired infinite feelings of joy, bliss, love, confidence, creativity, prosperity, abundance, and beauty. So what it means to get out of your way then? Stop trying to do something, or get something, or someone on the outside, and think that you need an intermediary to go to the source of true happiness, fulfilment, and who you indeed are. Required from you; is that you shed some of your old beliefs, habits, and rituals, and do less to get more. In this book, you will find my insights and experiences, stories and experiences of many of my coaching clients, and people I've met along my journey in the last 25 years. This book will mainly focus on why we do what we do instead of how we do it. There are countless

books out there on how to use strategies, techniques, and most don't work or produce limited, undesired, or unsustainable results. It's because of the missing link.
 In my experience, knowing why we do what we do is the missing link. When we truly understand and experience 'why,' it propels us to a deeper level of knowledge and understanding, and 'how-to' becomes natural, effortless, and sustainable.
When I work with my clients, I provide functional coaching and focus on finding the root cause of the problem. I don't focus on the symptoms, and focus on helping them release past traumas and past pains, usually within the first four sessions, and equip them with tools to practice at home, daily and consistently, to improve their emotional fitness and their lives.

Why we do; is the root cause of the problem that has been there probably since childhood. And what we do and how we do it are the symptoms. It is the emotional stress that produces thoughts. You can't just chant the pain away. You have to do the deep internal work. You cannot drink the pain away, or take drugs, food, or whatever other detrimental addictive behaviours to take the pain away. Whatever you do on the outside, will not take the pain away. It might temporarily; that is why we take drugs or consume alcohol because we are looking to numb the pain for some time. Unfortunately, this is not sustainable, and it could also be detrimental to our mental and physical health. There is no app for it either; you cannot press the button and use an app to take the pain away; unfortunately, it requires the deep internal work and for the pain to be seen and experienced.
It seems that for decades, self-limiting and self-destructive beliefs have brought us to this critical point in history. We stand on the brink of an unstable precipice, desperately hoping that things will get better. If we are to avoid this unstable and destructive future,

we must do something different. We, as individuals, are the solution to the problems we face together. We can do deep internal work and change self-limiting beliefs that are no longer worthy of who we are or who we are becoming, and create peace, harmony, and happiness in our lives. Think about it for a moment, all of the superstar celebrities that died young in the last few years: Amie Winehouse, Witney Huston, George Michael, Michael Jackson, Prince, Actor Robin Williams. Loved, idolised, and respected by millions of people around the world, and apparently, this wasn't sufficient for these superstars. It's known within the therapist community that all of these people suffered from the severe lack of deep, meaningful connection and they felt that they were not enough. They were continually rehearsing internally, "I am not enough." It's one of the most damaging affirmations one can affirm inwardly. No amount of external success, money, external love and fame can substitute internal self-love, self-worth, and self-respect. So next time you think about "One day when I ….. I will be happy" STOP….., and work on internal self. It is paramount to develop a deep connection, self-love, self-respect, self-worth, and self-confidence before you start working on acquiring material objects, pursuing your career goals, or looking for significant others to develop a deep, meaningful relationship.

We live in a world that has been programmed in fear. It is hard to escape because it's seen in almost everyone you interact with, and has become acceptable. It is hard to know the way out. From childhood on, this is the only world almost everyone knows. We are so easily influenced as a child, that we can't even see that it doesn't have to be this way. Each generation brings the next into this fearful world, blinded to the fact that there is a way out. So the next generation accepts that this is the way it has to be. It is a vicious cycle. We can put an end to the cycle and replace it with a world of unity, solidarity, kindness, compassion, gratitude, and love. You could have it all; you could be delighted and fulfilled every day, with who you are and how you are. You could have deep, meaningful relationships with yourself and others, develop deep self-love, and whatever your current situation - you too can turn your life around and have it all, including the relationship bliss. The quality of the relationship we have with ourselves, how we feel about ourselves, how much we like, love ourselves determines the quality of the relationships we have with others. If we desire a deep, meaningful relationship with a significant other, family, friend, coworker, we first have to develop a deep, meaningful relationship with ourselves. How we feel about ourselves, our thoughts, and daily internal dialogue create pictures and movies about ourselves. Research has found that most of us have a lot of negative thoughts, feelings, and have a daily negative inner dialogue, which has a detrimental impact on how we feel about ourselves and our relationships.

Stephen Hawking has a beautiful message for anyone who suffers from depression: "Remember to look up at the stars and not down at your feet. Try to make sense of what you see and wonder about what makes the universe exist. Be curious. And however difficult life may seem, there is always something you can do and succeed at. It matters that you don't just give up." As a man who overcame such incredible obstacles and lived such a brave and fantastic life, this advice couldn't come from a better place.

Health secrets for mind and body are not to mourn the past, worry about the future, or anticipate obstacles, but to live in the present moment wisely and earnestly.. We often feel the need to change the past or control the future, and we attempt to change something through worrying. Trying to change the past or the future is a deeply rooted cause of anxiety, which makes worrying an inner thing, not the result of an outside factor.

As Lao Tzu said, "If you are depressed you are living in the past. If you are anxious, you are living in the future. If you are at peace, you are living in the present."

Buddha said: "The trouble is, you think you have time'. But there is no time to waste: the past is gone, the future is not here yet, and all we have is the present".

Everyone worries. Conflict at work, a doctor's appointment that concerns you, or an exam that you need to take, can all be reasons to worry. The difference between thinking and worrying is that thinking leads to a solution, while worrying is an endless series of thoughts that keep going through your mind. 'What if this or that happens……?' 'Imagine if that……..?'
Worry, and anxiety about the future come in the form of negative mental rehearsal of the future vision, or even a movie associated with strong negative emotions felt in our body. This process often occurs under our conscious awareness, as a learned unconscious habit, and is something that we have been doing for years. We often behave and live by the set of negative thoughts, emotional reactions, and learned behaviours, all running like a computer program undetected, and under our conscious awareness.
I say to my coaching clients; it appears that you are playing a psychic. Do you have a Crystal Ball and can predict the future?
Why do you keep rehearsing a vision of the negative outcome and worry when you genuinely desire a positive outcome? What is the vision or the movie about your future that you can see?

If you are a psychic and can predict the future, surely you would start rehearsing vision and a movie with a positive outcome. You would choose to use your psychic crystal ball to see the vision of what you'd like to see (in the past tense), and that would be your daily movie, and positive mental rehearsal coupled with strong positive emotions and feelings.

The intent of most people who worry is probably to put their thoughts in order, get their head on straight. Or to prepare for a situation.

But nothing is less accurate: worrying does not lead to solutions or new insights. Much concern can lead to stress, anxiety, and gloom. Moreover, worrying takes a lot of time and energy. Marko Thum tells it; the present moment is all there truly is: "The present moment is the only thing where there is no time. It is the point between past and future. It is always there, and it is the only point we can access in time. In other words, between the past and the future, we have positive choices to make in the present moment." Everything that happens; only ever happens in the present moment. Everything that ever happened and will ever happen can only happen in the present moment. It is impossible for anything to exist outside of it.

When we engage in mindfulness or present moment meditation, we are not ignoring or denying thoughts of the past or future; we are simply choosing not to dwell on them. It's okay to acknowledge and label our past- and future-focused thoughts, categorise them, and be aware of their importance. When we are aware and present, we don't need to worry about getting caught up in thoughts of our past or anxiety about our future—we can revisit our past and anticipate what is to come without losing ourselves and our inner peace.

<u>Activity</u>

Have an inward experience and a new you will emerge.

When we focus our attention on our breath, we have no choice but to be in the present moment. To bring yourself back into the present, during the moment of stress or when you're feeling overwhelmed by the past or the future, you can try breathing ten deep breaths. Inhale deeply and slowly for 5 seconds and exhale slowly for 5 seconds, repeat ten times or more, keeping your attention on your breathing. Do this any time that need arises.

Chapter 3 - EMOTIONAL MUSCLES

In this chapter, I will talk about the benefits of emotional fitness. Still, before we dive into how to begin building the habits of emotional fitness, it's worth taking a closer look at the real-life benefits of doing so. Because the clearer we are on why emotional fitness will benefit us, the more motivation we'll have to work toward it. Developing strong emotional fitness decreases stress and overwhelm. Most people make the mistake of only trying to reduce stress once it's arrived. And while stress is occasionally unavoidable, the biggest reason we get stressed out and overwhelmed is that we're not very good at managing our stressors. Part of emotional fitness is learning what sorts of events and situations tend to produce stress in us. The more aware we are of the connection between certain triggers (stressors), and most importantly, our stress response, the more intelligent we can be about dealing with those stressors before they become stress. For example, many people experience chronic stress and overwhelm because they're not very assertive. They have a hard time asking for what they want and saying no to the things they don't. But at its core, assertiveness is not a communication issue; it's an emotional issue.

By developing a better relationship with emotions like anxiety and guilt, we can improve our ability to manage our stressors assertively, and prevent them from producing stress in the first place. Let us go back to the relationship you have with yourself. What kind of relationship do you have with yourself? How do you feel about yourself? Do you have a negative internal dialogue? Do you worry often? Do you hear the constant voice in your head talking to you? Do you have something in the back of your mind always that is bugging you, that you are trying to remember or forget? What is your routine when you wake up first thing in the morning? What do you do? Do you look at your phone, your emails, texts, and social media? Research has shown that a positive morning routine has a tremendously positive effect on your emotional fitness. How you view yourself, a relationship with yourself, feeling of self-love, and self-confidence.

◆ ◆ ◆

Try these two fun activities and observe how you feel.

Scenario 1:
Read this scenario and after you've read it close your eyes and imagine doing the following: First thing in the morning, as soon as I wake up, I check my phone, messages, emails, and social media. And compare me with everyone else. Comparing what they look like on their photoshopped photos, glamorising their fake perfect lives, and how many likes they have. Checking how many likes I got, not feeling good about myself because I didn't get many likes and comments on my photo that I posted yesterday. It's why I've decided that other people's opinions, of who I am, and how I am has a direct impact on how I am choosing to feel about myself today and every day. After you have finished using your phone and finished with negative self-talk, you get out of bed and look at yourself in the mirror and then think; I don't like this about myself, I don't like that about myself, I don't like my body, I don't like my hair or my face. I've put on a few pounds, and I could lose a bit of weight. After all of those detrimental activities first thing in the morning, you must be thinking and feeling, "I don't like myself," "I am not happy." Right!

Probably! How do you feel? Take peace of paper and describe how you feel.

Scenario 2:
Imagine the following scenario: Read first, close your eyes and imagine. As I open my eyes in the morning, I say the following: I am grateful for my breath, I am grateful for being alive, I am grateful for being healthy, I am grateful for being happy. I sit on the edge of my bed, close my eyes, and do 20 deep breaths, focusing on each deep inhale and each deep exhale. Or meditate for 5-10 minutes focusing on my breathing — more on meditation techniques in the later chapters.
After the breeding exercise or meditation; I keep my eyes closed and affirm the following: I am enough, I like myself, I love myself. I am loved, I am lovable, I am strong, I am beautiful, I am amazing, I am intelligent, I am powerful. Every day and in every way, I am getting better and better. Still keeping your eyes closed; visualise your perfect life. You have achieved all your dreams goals and desires; you look beautiful in the most beautiful outfit, you're living in a beautiful home, drive the car of your dreams, have a job or business of your dreams, and have a partner of your dreams. See yourself happy, successful, and fulfilled. See yourself in the life that you'd like to manifest in the near future as already happening; you are living this life right now but seeing it in the past tense. Now open your eyes and see how you feel? Do you feel better after the scenario 2? Most definitely! We have been programmed since our childhood to say negative affirmations to ourselves from the moment we wake up, all day, and every day. We do this often unconsciously. But if you only replace a few morning rituals, similar as in scenario 2, and do the positive affirmations and praise yourself, every day, for the next 90 days, you would benefit tremendously. You could find more positive rituals in the following

chapters. The mind is very powerful, and what we say to ourselves has a direct impact on how we feel about ourselves. We see everything in pictures and movies, and we attach an emotion to what we see and how we see ourselves.

Imagine you have a best friend that you like very much and every day you are insulting this friend. Imagine that you are saying hurtful, offensive things to your best friend; " I hate you" " You are not enough," "You are stupid," "You are an idiot," "Everyone is better than you," "You are a loser," "No-one loves you, and no-one ever will," "You are ugly and don't deserve to be loved."

Do you think your friend will stay around for a long time and take those insults? How long will your friend stay? What is an appropriate way to talk to you fried to strengthen and elevate the relationship?

Praise your friend, be kind, supportive, loving, and compassionate.

From now on; Talk to yourself as you would to your best friend or a spouse that you love.

Unless you get rid of your guilt feelings and cease belittling yourself for your imagined inadequacies, you will be one of those who continue the fruitless struggle to attain total self-confidence and personal freedom. In order to be truly happy, compassionate, warm, and loving, you must first begin by understanding and loving yourself. You have been told to, "Love thy neighbour as thyself," but until you have a full appreciation of who and what you are, and learn to love yourself truly it defrauds both you and your neighbour!

When you look around at your fellow human beings, you will find it hard to ignore the fact that very few people are profoundly happy, fulfilled, and lead purposeful lives. Most of them seem unable to cope with their problems and the circumstances of daily living. The majority, settling for the average, and have resigned themselves to "just getting by." Resignation to mediocrity has become a way of life. As a result, feelings of unworthiness cause them, quite humanly, to blame society, people, circumstances, and surrounding conditions for their failures and disappointments. The idea that people and things (externally) control their lives is so thoroughly indoctrinated in their thinking that they normally will not respond to logical arguments that prove otherwise.

"To believe that our life is controlled in any way by anything or anyone on the outside imposes a condition of mental slavery which makes us a prisoner by our own commandment."

Our thoughts and feelings become the blueprint, which attracts from the universe all the elements that go into fulfilling our concepts, whether they be positive or negative. What we have in our life right now is the outward manifestation of what has been going on inwardly. We have literally attracted everything that has come into our life, good or bad, happy or sad, success or failure. This includes all facets of our experience, including business, marriage, health or personal affairs. Think about it! Your surroundings, your environment, your world all outwardly picture what you think and feel about inwardly. By discovering why you are the way you are, you also find the key to being what you want to be.

THE POWER TO CHANGE

Does this describe you? Do you concentrate on your limitations, your failures, your blundering way of doing things, seldom stopping to think of what you might be? The problem is that you have been conditioned since childhood by false concepts, values and beliefs that have prevented you from realising how truly capable and unique you are.

By virtue of your role as co-creator of your life, you have the power to change any of its aspects. Every great teacher has come to the same conclusion: you cannot look to someone outside yourself to solve your problems. As the Master Teacher reminded us so often, "The Kingdom of Heaven is within." It is not in some distant land, and it is not up in the sky. Buddha came to the same realisation when he said, "Be a lamp unto your own feet and do not seek outside yourself." Self-healing powers are within. Health, happiness, abundance and peace of mind are natural states of being once you break the bonds of negative thinking.

Unless you perceive your own true worth as a person, you cannot come close to achieving total self-confidence. Only to the degree that you can truly acknowledge your own unique importance will you be able to free yourself from self-imposed limitations.

Yes, I said self-imposed! Our parents, our family, our boss or society didn't do it to us. We do it to ourselves by allowing others to control our lives.

As one sage puts it, "We aren't what we think we are, but what we think we are!" You are about to start on an adventure that will reward you for the rest of your life. You are going to learn new ways to break the bonds of limitations that have been holding you back. This book will provide a paradigm shift and open your heart to unlimited possibilities. If you find yourself in a situation where you seem to be going nowhere, feel inadequate, and unable to face life with enthusiasm and confidence, then continue reading. If you are disappointed by past results, and not content to drift through life, these pages offer you an alternative. If you allow yourself to be open and receptive to new concepts, values, ideas, and beliefs, you will discover why you should and how you can systematically reorganise your thought processes to awaken THE REAL YOU.

We can only change the world to the extent that we can change ourselves. We can only change ourselves to the degree that we become aware of our mistaken beliefs.Because one believes in oneself, one doesn't try to convince others. Because one is content with oneself, one doesn't need others' approval.
Because one accepts oneself, the whole world accepts him or her. Lao Tzu

Activity

 Guilt is the major part of our lives, it was learned since childhood, which runs undetected, and under our conscious awareness. To live a truly happy and fulfilled life, we must get rid of the guilt.
1. Write in a notebook, how many times today you have felt guilty feelings towards yourself.
2. How many times has someone else tried to make you feel guilty today?
3. How many times have you tried to make another feel guilty?
Continue this activity for the next 90 or until you eradicate the guilt out of your life.

Have an inward experience and a new you will emerge.

Chapter 4 - WHO AM I?

Throughout history, one of the most profound questions humankind has asked itself is the question of its true identity: Who am I?
In order to develop great relationships with yourself, first, you need to understand who you indeed are.

In order to honestly know, don't try to understand it intellectually, you have to experience it through meditation.
Everything you think that you are and what you identify with who you are may come as a surprise to you to learn that is not who you indeed are!

Who are you? Who is the voice inside your head having a constant dialogue with you? Who is the one witnessing the dialogue going on in your head? Who is a watcher and the observer behind your eyeballs?

STOP for the moment; Don't think about the pink elephant!
You are now thinking about the pink elephant, and having an internal dialogue; what pink elephant? What is he talking about? At the same time, a witness is observing a voice asking these questions.

Pose for the moment, don't read anymore, and do this exercise: Close your eyes and think of the pink elephant, now try to become aware of any other thoughts or voices. What do you hear, who is the one witnessing the thoughts and voices about the pink elephant?

I asked one of my clients, even though I knew everything about him as I was coaching him for several years.
Nick, a thirty-eight-year-old solicitor, responded; I am a solicitor. I said, no, you are not. Who are you? I am Nick. I am thirty-eight years old. I am a man. I am a son, and I am a father. I kept saying no, you are not.

I said if you are you now, as Nick, thirty-eight years old, man, solicitor, father to your children and son to your mother, who was you when you were ten years old?
How about when you were 15 years old?
Is it the same you or a different you?
Same me, Nick replied.
Remember when you were ten years old four foot five, and you looked at yourself in the mirror, who was the one observing you looking in the mirror? It was me. I was looking in the minor. How about now?
You are thirty-eight and six foot two looking at yourself in the mirror. Is it the same you or a different you? Same me, Nick responded.
How is it then that you from birth, and since you can remember has been the same you, only in several different bodies?
The real you; age five, age seven, and age ten remained the same as your human body was growing and changing over the years.
Your external body was growing and evolving visibly, but your real 'you' remained the same. Well, the real you does change and grow, but not in the same sense as your external human body.
The change and growth are more subtle and invisible to the naked eye.
When you change, improve, and grow, you change at your core, as the saying goes. The core, if you will, is your real you.

Most important question:
Who are you/Who am I?

Before you answer this question, here are some rules:
You cannot use any of these to describe yourself and
answer it;
Gender, young/old, rich/poor, job, education, ethnicity,
where you come from, religion, profession, political
views, your name, age, income, social status, your past
or your future. Think about this question for a moment
and try to answer: Who am I? Before I answer the
question, 'Who am I?' I'd like to discuss some of the
things you will find in this book. In this book, there are
many teachings and methods not to make us into
something that we are not, but rather to awaken us to the
truth of who we are! When one becomes conscious of
their own true nature, all of the old unkindness and
selfishness are dropped, and the pure light of loving-
kindness and selflessness shines forth in glorious
brilliance. The one who is unconditionally loving, and is
empty of self, does not have any further need for lists of
commandments. Or books of rules, since such one is
living in intimate harmony with the divine, and every act
flows from the well-spring of divine intent. On the
surface, each of us is separate, and we have our way of
life. But, in the depth of being, we are all One.

◆ ◆ ◆

Who am I? These are my answers to this question:
I am that I am, I am a soul having a unique, individual
human experience in this lifetime.
I am an indwelling being.
I am universal consciousness.
I am infinite love, kindness, compassion, benevolence.
I am one with the divine, and divine is everything.

The answer to the question 'Who am I?' is much more complex and cannot be expressed in a sentence or two. There were many scriptures written just trying to find the answer to this question.
On the other hand, the shortest, spiritual answer that you can get is, 'You are not only the body.'
There are, however, so many ideas as to what this other part is; what is your soul, or this 'rest' which is not the body?

The nonphysical phenomena of who we are. Nikola Tesla said: "The day science begins to study nonphysical phenomena, it will make more progress in one decade than it has in all the previous centuries of its existence."

It includes your past with your development from your birth until now, the impressions that others have left on you and your experiences, your present with your mind, your thoughts and your feelings today and of course also your future, the dreams, plans and wishes that you have. There is, however, a bit more to 'you,' which is even more difficult to express in words. If you understand this 'I,' this little word deeply, you would know what I mean. Feeling that you know who is you, gives you a peace of mind and heart.
This understanding is why spiritual leaders, religions, and many people have always recommended for everyone to find the answer to this question. The reality is, however, that there is nobody who can give you the answer for you. You may have heard a guru or master tell you that they would help you, but the reality is that you have to find the answer for yourself through deep internal experience, and during the practice of meditation.
Nobody else can tell you who you are because we are all unique, but also identical at the same time. I am

personally pessimistic that the mind can be used to figure out the answer to "Who am I?

While science refers to human beings as a biological organism, philosophers understood that this perspective isn't sufficient. Our body is changing continuously, yet we remain ourselves.

For example, it's claimed that every seven years, all the cells of our body are replaced, and they are entirely new. So the body I have now is not the body I had seven years ago, yet I remained. So what is this "I" that remained? The western philosopher John Locke argued that momentary thoughts are not consistent and change over time. They cannot be our identity since identity is something that must be consistent over time.

He suggested that what makes a person himself is a minimal amount of memory that must remain constant throughout his life. For example, I am myself and not another because I remember being myself as a little child, as a teenager, and as an adult. He termed this consistency of memory, "sameness of consciousness." But also, Locke's suggestion was disproved and insufficient since very young babies don't have a self-memory. The distinction between "myself" and "other" develops over time. Furthermore, most of us have no memories before a certain age (usually not before the age of two), yet it is absurd to claim that the baby that I was and the adult I am today are not the same people. So mind or memory cannot be our true identity, and this is the spot where western philosophy got stuck.

The answer to the question, Who am I? It is found in the east and known for thousands of years.

It does have a clear answer. This was known to several eastern philosophies, such as Advaita Vedanta and Jnana Yoga. However, this answer was reached through a meditative process of self-inquiry, and therefore, couldn't be easily explained to someone who hasn't experienced this process by themselves.

They claim that in the background of our mind exists an "observer" or "experiencer," which is constant and never changing. It observes and experiences our mind (our thoughts, emotions, and sensations), but it is not the mind. This is who we are.

The 'I' is not the body. The 'I' is not the mind.
- 'I' hear my thoughts
- 'I' experience joy (emotion)
- 'I' feel cold (sensation)

From these sentences, we can see that the 'I' is separate from the thoughts, emotions, or sensations. More accurately, there is a thought, emotion, or sensation, and there is 'I' that observes or experiences this particular thought, emotion, or sensation. In the background of our inner world exists another layer, the layer of awareness or experience. It has to be experienced (felt) and not understood intellectually. To experience, do the following exercise: Close your eyes and Imagine a house; it doesn't have to be a clear image, it could be a real house or cartoon or an emoji house, the important thing is that you will see something, even a blur. Now look at the image of the house in your head, do you see it?

If you do, ask yourself two questions:
1.   Who sees the image of the house?
2.   What is the thing that sees the image of the house?
If you have done the exercise correctly, you would see the image of the house. Now the answer to the first question is; 'I.' 'I' see the image of the house. What is the thing that sees the image of the house? It is certainly not the emotion or sensation, nor it is a thought. House is a thought, but the thing that sees the image of the house is

an observer, the experiencer. So the mind and the 'I' that observe and experience the image of the house are not the same. 'I' am not the mind. 'I' am the observer, the experiencer, the witness.

There is a word for what I call the experiencer and is Consciousness. The word Consciousness it's often used with different meanings like intelligence or thought. The definition of Consciousness is the state of being aware — the awareness.
Human Consciousness has been defined as awareness, sentience, a person's ability to experience and feel, but despite the vital role it plays in our lives and making us who we are; we actually know very little about how Consciousness works.
Interestingly consciousness/awareness is making us who we are, but we as humans know little about how it works.

Q. Who am I?
A.   I am consciousness/awareness.

How do I become aware of my Consciousness? You begin by looking at yourself deeply, clearly, and carefully. The question "What am I"arises. The answer is, you are carrying around three components; mind and its' thoughts, your emotions and their feelings and your body and it' sensations.
These three components make up what we call the Ego, and it keeps us from experiencing who we really are because the Ego keeps us playing a social role, and projecting an image of ourselves to the world.
EGO = Edge God Out.

Now the question arises who am I, who carries these components, and it's aware that they are not you, even though at times it seems like they are.

You now begin to witness, study, and watch your mind and its thoughts, your emotions and their feelings, and your body and its sensations, and as you do, it becomes more apparent and more evident that they are not you but parts of your makeup. You begin to wonder more and more; well, if I am not those components, "WHAT AM I?" With constant vigilance of your mind, emotions, and body, you find yourself experiencing your REAL SELF, YOU, and that is what you are. You then begin to work on self- control. That is, you start taking control of your mind, emotions, and body.

Our experience of ourselves is similar to the one you have at the cinema while watching a movie. Remember the times you have been deeply immersed in the movie, and you are experiencing the film as real. You are laughing, crying, or feeling frightened, and then you realise that you just saw that actor on the screen, and you break free from the movie and find yourself sitting in the seat, observing the screen unemotional and detached. Congratulations, you have become the observer, and are back to being yourself. That's what happens when you get caught in your thoughts and feelings, and they become your reality and control you. The trick is to break free of your thoughts and emotions and become the observer of them, and detached from them so that YOU are in control of your life. As you do this, you begin experiencing the experience of profound HAPPINESS and FULFILMENT COMING FROM WITHIN.

Try these exercises to break free of your mind and its' thoughts.
Sit quietly in meditation, starting with ten deep breaths, focus on your breathing at first, and then observe your mind, bring your attention to your body and observe any emotions. As you become aware of your thoughts, and

with a regular daily practice of meditation, you will
achieve control of your unwanted thoughts and
emotions. You do this by focusing your attention on a
thought or symbol that you do not have an emotional
reaction or attachment to and when your mind takes you
away from that thought, you immediately return to
thinking the thoughts you want to think about.
In the beginning, you will find this very difficult
because your mind's (and ego's) job is to control you and
keep you from seeing and experiencing your Real Self,
who you really are. Since it has controlled you for so
long with no resistance from you, it is challenging to
break its grip, but with persistence, will power, and
patience you will find that when your thoughts take your
attention away from the thought you want to focus on, it
becomes easier and more comfortable to bring your
focus back to what you want to think. You begin to
experience with more clarity the feeling of being
yourself, observing your mind and thoughts that have
been controlling you. You begin to realise more and
more that you are not your mind, and arrive at a place
that not only does it not control you, but it also does not
affect your decision making at all. When your mind goes
quiet, you begin to hear THE STILL SMALL VOICE
WITHIN that is always talking to you and guiding you
but is usually drowned out by the loud and intoxicating
voice of the mind.
How many times have you thought to do something and
heard the small voice say you shouldn't, but you do it
anyway and then think, "I knew I shouldn't have done
that" or when you feel that your keys are in the car just
before you slam the door. That's the voice I am talking
about. It will guide you in every decision, and every
word you speak. You just go with the flow and its'
guidance. It will also guide you in better understanding
of your makeup, and lead you to Self- Realisation.

When you achieve thoughtless awareness, you experience living in the present moment and not in the future, which is your imagination, and not in the past, which is your memory. Experience inner peace, which is beyond words and can only be experienced and not comprehended or described. You are experiencing the Infinite HAPPINESS THAT LIES WITHIN.

Your Real Self is YOU. This Real Self that I am talking about is what you experience when you are not caught up in your Ego, which is your mind and emotions.

You have experienced yourself many times and didn't think about it that way. You just knew that you were more peaceful, content, and living in, and enjoying the moment.

Since your mind is not thinking for you, you find yourself thinking very clearly about your life. Some people have the experience of their Real Self when they are driving, and just focusing on the road. Listening to music or exercising brings some people back to their Real Self. Sometimes you just forget about your problems and stop thinking about them, and you are there. The aim is to stay there all the time, no matter what's going on in your life on the outside. This state it's called being centred or in the zone.

It means we are anchored in both spirit and mind, logic and emotion, physical reality and the ethereal world. Being centred describes being in balance between these two seemingly disparate parts of ourselves. When 'centred' we are our authentic self, in our personal lives and at work. We are true to ourselves, connected, non-judgemental, non-attached, and emotionally grounded.

Research tells us that regular meditation or mindfulness practise decreases the volume in the area of the brain responsible for fear, anxiety, and stress. The moment you start watching the thinker, a higher level of consciousness becomes activated. You then begin to

realise that there is a vast realm of intelligence beyond thought, that thought is only a tiny aspect of that intelligence. You also realise that all the things that truly matter - beauty, love, creativity, joy, inner peace - arise from beyond the mind. You begin to awaken.
If you are able to stay alert and present in the Now and watch whatever you feel within, rather than be taken over by it, it affords an opportunity for the most powerful spiritual practice, and a rapid transmutation of all past pain becomes possible. When you've understood the basic principle of being aware as the watcher of what happens inside you - and you "felt" it by experiencing it - you have at your disposal the most potent transformational tool.

Activity

Practice meditation for 90 days twice a day, in the morning, and last thing before bed. Start with 10 minutes each time you meditate and increase the time by 2 min each day until you arrive at one hour. Practising one to two hours of meditation each day will improve your life beyond recognition in every aspect. All the top achievers (who are also profoundly happy and fulfilled) meditate every day for one or two hours.

Chapter 5 - THE UNIVERSE

I hope by now you have tried meditation and began to have an experience of the part of the universe residing within you. The universe?.......... Yes, the universe; you are made out of the same stuff as the universe, and the more you do deep internal work, the more you connect to unlimited possibilities of co-creating with the universe. The universe is always co-creating through you, and you have probably been unaware of this most of your life.

Don't try to understand the above intellectually with your logical mind.

In order to understand it; you need to have an experience. And don't just try to meditate one time and only have one experience and say; this new age fluffy stuff doesn't work, I tried meditating once, and it didn't work. Eldin is full of shit........., I can't believe I wasted ten minutes of my life on this mumbo jumbo!?

To know (have an experience) with certainty that you are part of the universe. Part of the infinite love, health, intelligence, creativity, and infinite abundance, you need to have at least 90 experiences for one hour each day. You cannot understand this intellectually, you must have an inward experience. Consecutively over the next 90 days, and I promise you that you will love it so much, that you'll start meditating for even 2 or 3 hours a day, and will continue for the rest of your life.

Today in my meditation I released something, and actually, I came up with something, and I wanted to share with you. Would you like to make more money?

Would you like to have better relationships? If you are not in a relationship, would you like to have one where you find the right compatible partner who will love you unconditionally every day? Would you like to experience profound self-love?

The kind of love that is overflowing from within, like from the fountain of love and everyone looks at you and says, omg, you look amazing, you look so attractive, you are full of health and vitality, did you change your hair, did you lose weight?

Would you like to live from this place with unlimited possibilities, infinite confidences, infinite love, and endless abundance? Wouldn't it be great to live from this place; from the place where everything is unlimited?

The place where you have an infinity of abundance, money, love, confidence, self-esteem, creativity, where you have a direct connection to infinite intelligence, and a direct link to unlimited creativity.

The place where you are living more from your heart daily.

Wouldn't it be great to not only say deep down inside I know I will be okay? What if we live from this place permanently every day? I know I have said many times in the past; deep down inside, I know I will be okay. And this was when there was some stress in my life, some loss, some major challenge, trauma, like a break-up, loss of finance, business struggles, bereavement when my father passed away. So these are the moments when we all know with certainty that deep down inside, it's the place that exists within all of us, and from this place, we know that we will be okay, no matter what are the external circumstances. How and why do we all struggle to live from deep down inside every single day? The place where we only visit when we have some challenges in our life, when there is a crisis? Wouldn't it be great to live from this place 24/7?

That this is the only place that we can visit and live from, to create from, two love from, to feel the confidence from, to feel infinite abundance from, and to manifest the infinite abundance in our external lives. What came up in my meditation, that from now on, I am going to be making videos weekly and posting ideas and insights that they come up in my meditation to share with the world. Mind you, I had never made videos before, had zero experience, and was very shy and nervous. The first time I made a video of about 30 minutes long, I felt like I had a panic attack in the first 10 minutes of recording. I have experience and am comfortable with public speaking and presenting in front of a large group of people but have never made any videos, and I was extremely nervous.

How the inspiration for making the video unfolded? During my one hour meditation and at around 40 min mark, I just experienced the surge of inspiration and creative ideas coming through. And as soon as I finished the meditation I recorded a video, saying things in one take, with no script and unedited, I uploaded it to my YouTube channel. I felt like I was a conduit for the universe to channel this information through me. While I was speaking the words, 'watcher' me was listening and learning about the information that I had just spoken about for half an hour.

Since then, I have made several other videos unscripted, unprepared, and they get uploaded without any editing. The information was coming through me as a conduit, and if I wanted to think with my brain how to say and what to say, it would probably take me several days of trial and error. I would probably spend several days of editing and trying to make it (what society calls) perfect. But this information came through me, (not from me) from the higher place. From the place that we can all access.

It's free and available to access any time you desire.

 I am so grateful for the timeless, universal knowledge to pass through me and I surrendered fully to the unlimited possibilities of being a conduit and allowing the universe to channel through me without questioning why or how. I have had many similar experiences in the past, but I always thought it is just an idea, and sometimes I used to execute on it. But since I have fully surrendered, to be used by the universe as a conduit, countless other creative projects and creative ideas came through me since my first video, including this book that you are reading. Many great business ideas for my coaching business came through as well as my property investment business, and not to mention numerous amazing ideas on how to improve myself in every area of my life.

One of the ideas that came up in my meditation it's the name of the business 'The World Changers,' so not just myself, but I'd like to invite all of you to join me on this beautiful journey that we together can change the world. And it starts with the one; it starts from within each and every one of us. The idea is that as we as individuals are changing in a positive way from within, through the practice of meditation, other positive daily rituals, and this will have a positive ripple effect on everyone around us. So I thought 'The World Changers' was best suited. As I included all of you; we could contribute positively to our higher self and make a massive positive impact on humanity and the world.
If we stop focusing our attention on what is wrong with the world, and with the people around us and divert our entire focus on working on improving ourself inwardly for 90 days, one year, two years, or however long it takes, we will enhance our lives exponentially and as a result we would change the world.

When we connect deeper inwardly in our hearts, we generate the connection to the infinite source of abundance, infinite health and healing powers, an endless source of creativity, endless intelligence, self-confidence, and infinite self-love.

From this place, all of us feel deep in every cell, and our hearts right thing to do, be, say, and how to behave.
When we contribute from this place, we experience coincidences, synchronicities, and miraculous serendipities. We manifest beautiful abundance in our external life.
When we contribute and create from this place we experience effortless manifestation of plethora of abundance, health, love, creativity, inspiration, money, confidence, euphoric self-love, and love for other human beings, for all creation, for animals, for plans and we begin to live like nature, we live in cooperation, effortlessly creating and co-creating with the universe.
And things appear in our life easily and quickly, and everything seems so effortless.
The saying goes; when we change the energetic vibration on the inside, the vibration on the outside changes. We send through our hearts the emotional feelings of what we like to see manifest in our external life, and we send magnetic waves through our heart to the universe, and we feel it as already manifested.
When we say my heart is not in it, I am not feeling it. We might be trying to do something, but at the same time, we listen to our hearts' guidance, and how we feel. Our primary focus should be to observe how we feel, and not how we think; thoughts genuinely have very little power.
The science confirms that our world is made of electrical and magnetic energy — the atom.
And science says that if you change electrical or the magnetic field, you change that atom.

There is one organ in our body that produces the strongest electrical field and the strongest magnetic field. It's our heart.

The human heart is a producer of the strongest electrical and magnetic fields in the body. Our brain does as well, but the heart produces an electrical field 100 times stronger than the brain. The heart's magnetic field is 4,000 times stronger than the brain's magnetic field. What has been written about for thousands of years in ancient texts, science now confirms it. Our heart is the source of the universal language. Belief is the code that translates the possibility into reality in our world.

As science confirms it, all possibilities already exist! In the quantum field of infinite possibilities, you are already healed! Peace has already happened. Joy is already everywhere.

With our mind, we think of the perfect relationship, perfect job, income, life, and with our heart, we give that possibilities life.

Through the feeling in our hearts, we make it real in our world. Belief is the bridge between thought and emotion. We don't speak the words because the universe connects to the language of the heart, rather than the words we recite or affirm in whatever language we speak. It is not essential to actually recite and pray and ask for things that you desire to manifest into your external reality; you need to feel it in your heart. You need to send the correct magnetic energy from your heart, which is 4,000 times stronger than your brain's magnetic energy.

In other words, if we think, affirm, pray to make one hundred thousand pounds, and at the same time we send the emotion from our heart of worry and disbelief, we will never get it. So once the thoughts, feelings, and emotions become one, and if everything you desire, feel in your heart as if you already have in abundance. You feel this deep in every cell of your body. The universe feels this emotional, energetic, and magnetic vibration, and it makes it appear quickly and effortlessly in your physical reality. So that is how quickly and easily things manifest.

You probably know about the law of attraction as many people have written about it, spoken about it, and they always published a lot of missing links. It is not sufficient to just sit and visualise and write down your goals. The missing link is the feelings and the emotions transmitted from your heart.

Some people call it intention. But underneath the intention is positive energy from your heart, feeling as if everything has already been accomplished.

What it means to feel and experience the infinite abundance and endless possibilities, is to feel and surrender that the universe indeed has an infinite abundance. Emitting positive energy form your heart is trusting that the universe has endless possibilities

When you decide on your goal that you have written down and connected with the intense emotions and feelings as goal already manifested right now. And the more you live as though everything you are desiring has already manifested. The more you live from the place of infinite abundance from within, universal unlimited possibilities, the things you desire manifest quickly and effortlessly.

You shouldn't try to figure out with your mind how the universe is going to make things manifest for you. The more you think how and when, and the more you worry, the longer it will take for things to manifest. Don't try to understand it or conceptualise it.

Our brains and bodies are finite with minimal knowledge and have only been on this planet for a split second, compared to the universe that has been in existence for probably infinite number of years.

You need to trust and surrender to the powers of universal consciousness that reside within you. And your job is to create through your heart and your emotions. It's the only universal language that the universe understands.

It is not good enough for you to write down the goals and desire some material object, a new sports car, but at the same time, your vibrational energy, your emotions, and your feelings are contradictory to the goal you desire.

Your goal is to get a new sports car for £100,000, but your emotions and your feelings are saying I don't deserve it.

Your hart is emitting: I will never be able to get it, I don't deserve it, and you have negative emotions and feelings. The universe does not listen to the words you speak or your thoughts but listens to the emotions and feelings you are sending.

I want the Porsche Carrera, but my heart is emitting 4,000 times stronger vibration; I don't deserve it. Listen to your heart, and work on changing your vibration, not your goal.

When you see a confident person, you feel their confidence oozing from within. It has very little to do with the way they look or their outfit.

◆ ◆ ◆

If you can't afford to pay your rent, work on your heart,
change your vibration,
and you'll elevate your life exponentially.

◆ ◆ ◆

So you can pray all you want, you can write as many goals as you wish. You can close your eyes and visualise the goals manifesting. But if you don't address your emotional fitness first, and if you don't get your emotions and feelings to be in alignment with your

thoughts of your goals, you will not be able to manifest them.
The universe doesn't know the difference between £1 and £1 million. It is you who has negative emotional resistance about the £1 million.
Try this:
1. Think of manifesting £1, what are your emotions and feelings, how do you feel? Relaxed, it's easy.
2. Think of manifesting £1 million, what are your emotions and feelings, how do you feel? Not relaxed; if you are honest with yourself, you probably feel some negative emotions, resistance, and or fear?

You are thinking about your next goal. New car, one million pounds, doubling your profit in your business, ask for a pay rise. A goal to come up with the next £100 million business idea, ideal partner, improve your health and fitness, lose weight. You want to make an extra £1,000 a month, or you want to move to a new home. Whatever your goal is, it's not essential the size or the number. Still, if you do not align your emotions and your feelings with your thoughts, the goals will not manifest in the physical reality, they might manifest to a degree but not entirely.

People go around saying, first, I have to see it to believe it.
But everything that exists in this world was invented and created as a first, buy a human being. It never existed before this first inventor had an idea and developed it. The chair you are sitting on, the device you are using to read this book (if it's Kindle), was created as a first before it ever existed. There are so many things that humans believe in that don't understand how they work. If you want to have light in your home at night, you have to turn the switch on even though you might not

know how electricity works. You use your smartphone every day without needing to understand how it works first.

The process of creating and manifesting happens in reverse; first, you must surrender and believe, and then you will see it. If you find it difficult to surrender and believe, it's because you have been living in lack, limitation, fears, and phobias most of your life.

Let's say the goal is to create an additional £5,000 per month income, but your emotions and feelings are contradictory to your goal. And you might be feeling; I don't deserve it, I will never be able to make it, I am not good enough, etc. So you continue working hard, and the work you are producing is not in alignment with your thoughts of an additional £5,000 per month. But with your negative, opposing emotions and feelings you only produce the quality of work that will pay an additional £800 per month instead of £5,000.
And then you settle for this, thinking I should have worked harder, perhaps if I implement new strategies and techniques I'd be able to achieve the goal of an additional £5,000 next month.
You continue looking externally for what you need to do or have, to achieve this goal. But this goal or any other goals will continue to be challenging to accomplish if you don't do the necessary deep internal work and align your emotions and feelings with your thoughts and the goal as though it has already manifested. When you do this, now you begin to talk, to act, to behave, to create, to produce as a person who has an additional £5,000 per month, and the goal manifests effortlessly.
How quickly, easily, and effortlessly the goal manifests entirely depends on how quickly and easily you embody positive feelings and emotions about the goal and feel in

your heart that it is possible and that you are the source of the infinite abundance and unlimited possibilities.

So it's not even that important to have a clear goal or to have a deadline. Still, it is paramount to do deep internal work and to remove any emotional blockages which stop you from feeling the emotions and feelings necessary to achieve and manifest these goals into your life. If you want to achieve something in the next six months, you first need to work on yourself internally and build a solid foundation. You first need to change your emotional vibration from within.
Feel in your heart with the certainty that this is already manifested today in your physical reality. You live this every single day, and you behave like this, you talk like this, you energetically vibrate as though everything you wanted has already manifested. It's how you create, and this is the language of the Universe, which is the emotions and feelings — another reason why it is so important to practice emotional fitness daily. Improving your emotional fitness should be the primary goal and the foundation for being and creating anything in life. The meditation is your shortcut to improving your emotional fitness.

If you are a kind of person, who is going to ask, so what do I get from meditation? Why should I meditate?

Daily practice of meditation is the quickest and best way to improve your emotional fitness and also a direct connection to the universe. Meditation will help you remove/release any old traumas, pains, blockages, and you will get connected deeper into your heart. The deeper you connect to your heart, the stronger your emotional fitness, happier and more fulfilled you will feel.

Activity

Try this fun game to manifest anything easily and quickly.

Meditate daily for ninety days for an hour or two, and during meditation practice visualising your goals as they have already manifested, and you are looking at them in the past.

Example: I enjoyed driving my new car (describe it) to Paris last month (explain what you been doing, where you've stayed etc.) and say it all in the past tense.

Meditate, visualise, write, and speak in the past tense about your goals and feel the positive feelings and emotions if you want to manifest anything in your life quickly and easily.

Do this for a year every day (one or two hours a day), and your life will improve exponentially.

Chapter 6 - CONDUIT OF UNIVERSAL CONSCIOUSNESS

Emotional fitness is paramount to align your vibrational energy with the universal power of whatever you are trying to manifest. First you have to meditate for an hour or two every day. In the second step, you have to improve your emotional fitness, your feelings, and emotions. Emotions have to be aligned with the goal that you're trying to achieve as though you already have it right now. See it, feel it, and experience it in the past tense.

Each time you meditate, you are sending your emotions and feelings into the universe, and you say thank you. You express gratitude, you write down a gratitude list for the goals as already manifested and feel it deeply and emotionally. Visualise the outcome as already manifested. You say, thank you for my incredible car, thank you universe, thank you, god, whatever you want to call it. God, the universe, divine source, Jesus, Energy, universal consciousness , whatever you want to call it. It is the same thing whether you're Christian, Muslim, Buddhist, Jewish, or Atheist. Whatever your religious beliefs are, it's one and the same; the source, the creation of everything including you and I.
It's actually a creation of this book, I am just a conduit and the book was just coming through me and had begun coming through me during one of my hour-long meditation sessions, and had written itself effortlessly. I feel that it happened when I started to surrender to who I

truly am and without needing to understand it or conceptualise it intellectually.

When I surrendered, the universe started channeling fantastic creative things, through me, and I have grown and expanded from within so much, beyond recognition. When I first started experiencing all of these tremendous creative expansions from within, often creative ideas that I have never thought about, or studied and at first it was so mind-boggling that I was trying so hard to understand where they are coming from. When I surrendered to the possibility that I am a conduit and that the universe is co-creating through me, I started to experience an avalanche of most amazing creative ideas surging so powerfully from within. Like my heart would be on fire until I express these ideas on paper, audio, or video, and afterward, I would feel such a deep inner peace and bliss like I have never felt before. The more I did this, the more universe used me as a conduit to channel some of the most incredible ideas, projects, next big inventions, or the next billion pounds idea.

Most importantly, throughout the entire process, I would feel deep euphoric self-love surging from within like a fountain, and would continue to feel the same even after the meditation, as I am working, interacting with people, and going about my day to day activities. I realised that I became so connected to my heart, and I felt so open and free to be vulnerable and connected to everyone and everything around me.
Emotions and feelings are most important in the manifestation of everything, and the thoughts are secondary. Your thoughts have no power whatsoever on your life, on who you are, on how you are. Everything we do, how we behave, how we interact with others stems from the emotions and feelings we experience in our bodies.

Most people spend their entire life never training their emotional fitness to be able to live a healthy, profoundly happy, and fulfilled life. And most are not even fully aware of their emotions and feelings, let alone the requirement for daily positive rituals to improve their emotional fitness.
Most people learn that negative emotions are wrong, and we have to run away from them, avoid them, and suppress them.

One of the leading causes of many psychological problems is the habit of emotional avoidance. It could seem surprising because the attempt to avoid negative emotions appears to be a reasonable thing to do.
As we know, negative emotions don't feel good, and they are often linked in our minds to adverse events that we want to avoid or forget. Besides, we are all familiar with the momentary relief that avoidance can provide. If the thought of speaking up upsets me, then I can make myself feel better by deciding not to speak. Indeed, avoidance is an effective solution in the short term.
Long term, however, it becomes a bigger problem affecting your mental and physical health than whatever was being avoided in the first place.

People in the UK generally don't like to talk about topics relating to mental health, emotions, and feelings. Some people would rather go down to the pub and have a few drinks to numb the pain and hide their true emotions and feelings, then acknowledge them and do the deep internal work that it requires. And then starting from Thursday binge drink after work, try to call in sick on Friday, or turn up to work still intoxicated, binge drink on a Friday, and Saturday, spend on average 10 hours on weekends watching their favourite shows, spend 20 hours a week scrolling aimlessly through social media, or do other addictive activities to give them temporary relief.

Suppressing and avoiding a negative emotion buys you short term gain at the price of long term pain. In the long run, however, you will develop a bigger problem (addiction), in addition to the unresolved issues you had avoided by drinking or doing other detrimental activities.

We often worry and have a need to be sure about our future, but no amount of analysis and theories can give you the certainty that you are looking for because no one truly knows anything, including yourself, about how your life is going to turn out.

The truth is uncertainty should be our friend, and the truth is we don't know anything, we don't know what's going to happen tomorrow, we cannot predict the future, there is no past, and there is no future; it's all an illusion. All we have is the present moment, all we have is now, and the more we experience from the now, and we feel centred and balanced in the now the better quality of life we will have.

No one truly knows anything or can present factual evidence with certainty about what's going to happen tomorrow, a few weeks from now, months, or years from now about your personal life.

You spend most of your time worrying and look at external possibilities of an outcome, but ultimately what you are desiring, is the need to know with certainty that you are going to be okay and that you will not experience any pain or suffering.

What everyone is looking for; is the certainty that they will feel okay. They will feel peace, bliss, profound love, happiness, and fulfilment.

People say; hey, I want to enjoy my life. What they're talking about is the entertainment, they are talking about having fun, but those are just external activities, that could be fun for a short period.

Ultimately what we are looking for it's the internal feelings that those activities produce. Still, when we feel the temporary feelings of joy, happiness, love, confidence, which are not sustainable, we keep going for more external activities or detrimental addictions to experience these feelings.

But the only sustainable feeling of joy, happiness, love, bliss, confidence can be achieved when we go deep internally and do the deep internal work.

When we start doing deep internal work, we will notice some pains and blockages that we experience in our bodies, and we might have an urge to understand them, fix them, and remove them somehow. Negative emotions and feelings may not be fun, but they are not bad, and they will not kill you if you acknowledge them, and feel them deeply.

Feeling deep and acknowledging the negative emotions and feelings, loosens their strength, and the perceived pain or destructive power.

We're not supposed to be doing anything; we sit there to acknowledge them, and they are going to begin to dissolve; that's all that is required is to bring to our awareness that we are here seeing them and acknowledging them. Just be a space for your traumas, pain, and insecurities and acknowledge them, and ultimately, when we do this, they will begin to dissolve.

These feelings and emotions we experience in our bodies, with a physical sensation, and the intensity of the sensation varies and fluctuates depending on what we are doing to distract ourselves from feeling and experiencing them fully.

These physical sensations, traumas, pains are linked to our childhood, and it's usually our five-year-old inner child that feels the pain and who needs to be seen and acknowledged.

This pain or trauma might be something as small as; Mother or Father told us something when we were five years old, and we perceived it as being told that we are not good enough. And now that we are adults 20, 30, 40, 50, 60 or older we still feel the pain or trauma that we have been holding onto unconsciously for all these years seeking approval from our parents, trying to prove to them that we are good enough and we just want to be loved.
Our five-year-old inner child is saying I want to be held, and I just want to be loved. I'd like you to acknowledge me, please.
My mother always told me that I need to make her proud and that I need to become something. I need to do something or have something so she can be proud of me.

All of these things are very deep down inside, and people don't want to experience them. They go through life doing so many unhealthy, detrimental things to numb the pain. They think that if I feel and experience the pain, oh my god is going to kill me. The pain is saying, please see me, please, it's your five-year-old who just fell scraped its knee. And saying please feel me, please see me, cuddle me, hold me, and kiss me.

What do you do if you can travel back in time and see your five-year-old self fall? What would you do? Would you shout, would you hit your five-year-old self, scream and tell them that they are not good enough, or would you say; it's ok darling come here let me cuddle you, let me hold you tightly. You'd tell them that you love them,

and that is all that the pain requires. It doesn't need you to fix it, to judge it, to remove it somehow.
It just needs you to experience it fully.
You might need to cry for a few minutes, a few days, for a few months. It doesn't matter if you cry, that's how you release it.
You see it, experience it, feel it, you give it love, and it starts to dissolve. It might come back because this is a habitual process you've been having.
You've been habitually experiencing this emotional trauma for so many years, so it might take a little bit longer for you to do certain practices to remove it, and release it.
But at the beginning of the process, you make it your best friend. If you have children, you know what I'm saying.
The kind of love that your five-year-old self needs, it was the same when you had your first child, those first few seconds that you held your baby in your arms, and you gave it so much unconditional love, that is the kind of love you need to give it. Your five-year-old self requires that kind of love. You provide it this kind of love, and it begins to dissolve, you begin to open your heart, and you begin to feel so much better, and so much lighter.
You feel the release, and now you start to notice that you don't need substances.

You don't need to abuse yourself. People say substance abuse. It's not substance abuse; it's self-abuse.
The substances people consume, or loads of unhealthy food, loads of drugs, loads of alcohol, they gamble or do other things to take their pain away. To give them this positive feeling, the endorphins experience, so they can bury the emotion of the pain and trauma deeper and deeper, and suppress it.
The more they do this, the pain intensifies.

The more you try to ignore it, the more you trying to hide away from it, the more you try to run away from it, it intensifies.

At the beginning you might be drinking a glass of wine a day, the pain is it not been or experienced, you now feel further pain even after a glass. Now, you need two drinks, and soon you need a bottle, then you start taking some drugs. You begin to consume more addictive detrimental substances and abuse yourself more. People say; I have a high tolerance, so I have to consume more.

You first started taking a small amount of drugs for the pain that you wanted to dissolve, hide away from, or suppress. Now your system has gotten used to it. This pain is powerful. It's emotional pain, the emotional suffering for twenty or thirty years that you have not addressed. The pain that you tried to bury for years. It's coming up; it's more potent than any drug, so you take more drugs, do more detrimental things. You try running, but it's like running away with a parachute that is attached to you, and it's pulling you back. It has been attached to you for decades. You can't get rid of it. The faster you run, the more is pulling you back and giving you pain and giving you suffering.
You cannot run away from that, cannot suppress it by consuming various detrimental substances. Detrimental to your mental and physical health. Often more detrimental fo your mental health, which is less visible but more damaging.
But the only way you can achieve a sustainable feeling of profound joy, happiness, love, bliss, confidence can be achieved when we go deep internally and do the deep internal work.
When we start doing deep internal work, we will notice some pains and blockages that we experience in our bodies, and we might have an urge to understand them,

fix them, and remove them somehow. Negative emotions and feelings may not be fun, but they are not bad, and they will not kill you if you acknowledge them, and feel them deeply.

Feeling deep and acknowledging the negative emotions and feelings, loosens their strength, and the perceived pain or destructive power.
If your adult self could travel back in time and see your little five-year-old child self fall, hurts their knee, bleeding, and crying in pain, would you ignore it or scream and shout at it? You wouldn't, would you?
It just needs to feel seen, acknowledged, needs hugs, and to be held for a few moments tightly and to feel safe, needs kisses, and needs to feel loved.
So next time you feel the pain, you feel the physiological discomfort inside of your body; you say inwardly, and I love that.

First, allow yourself to fully see it, feel it, acknowledge it, then open your heart fully and give it the most significant, tightest hug and send more love than you have ever done before.
Practice this every day during meditation, and any times that need arises.
You've tried running away from it, tried to ignore it, tried to numb the pain with various detrimental addictive behaviours, and your inner five-year-old child has been crying and suffering in pain, feeling neglected and abandoned. All it ever wanted is to be acknowledged and loved unconditionally.
Your task is not to try to fix it, judge it, understand it, or try somehow to remove it but to feel it fully, experience it, become aware of it entirely and profoundly, and give it unconditional love, hold it tightly, and give it hugs and kisses.

Some people feel it in their stomachs, heads, throats, chest, or all over the body as tightness, pressure, and pain, but wherever you feel your inner child suffering in pain, all it wants is to bee seen and loved unconditionally.
My clients ask me, after acknowledging their inner five-year-old child and experiencing the pain, the following question. Do I go and speak to my parents and tell them how I feel?
And I'd say, why do you feel the need to tell them how you feel?
Now that I know what they've done to me, I need to tell them how I feel, they'd say. Why do you have the need to do that, I'd ask?
Because after I tell my parents how I feel, they could apologise, and I could feel better, they'd say.

There is a general misconception that we need someone on the outside to apologise or behave in a certain way for us to be happy. Every time we feel and think like this, we give another power over us. Our emotions are experienced internally, and the relationship we have with our parents is experienced internally. Often if we confront our parents or another, they will probably be oblivious to how we feel and what they might have done something wrong and that they'd need to apologise.
If you feel the need to talk to your parents and express how you feel, do it for you and get it off your chest if you must, but don't insist that your parents apologise. If they volunteer an apology, great, but don't insist on getting one. You need to practice forgiveness and release from within.
When my clients practice meditation, acknowledge their five-year-old child, and practice other positive rituals for a while, to release the pain and trauma, they tell me that they don't need to talk to their parents, or ex-spouse, or anyone else from their past.

The purpose of doing the deep internal work is to claim your power; you will feel more self-love, self-confidence, freedom, inner peace, joy, and profound happiness and fulfilment.
After a short time, some people begin to feel the deep sensation of release and feel lighter and open. Some clients have told me that they felt like their heart had opened up fully, and they felt the courage to feel vulnerable and let people in, as they began to feel profound self-love and self-confidence. Habits make you the person you are. It is impossible to make a significant change in your life without destroying the compulsive hold they have upon you. Unless you are happy, healthy, calm, peaceful, self-reliant, and successful in every area of your life, changing self-defeating habits must be a priority in your life.
Most of us have no idea how much our lives are built around so-called "bad habits." We have programmed the wrong responses into our subconscious minds and central nervous system. It causes us to respond the way we have conditioned ourselves to feel and act, no matter how negative false, distorted, or destructive this might be. Consequently, we must go through a period of unlearning or deprogramming to change our negative, self-defeating habit patterns.

Activity

For the next 90 days, practice going inwardly, feeling deeply, and if you encounter any pain or discomfort, give it love and say, I love that. Commit to eradicating any negative detrimental habits and replace them with positive.

Chapter 7- I AM

"Being confident and feeling good about yourself is not
a luxury;
it is an absolute necessity!"

Express what you feel to be true, remember whatever
you attached to 'I am,' you become. I am, which means
indwelling being, life awareness unconditioned
consciousness, self-originated spirit. Before any
manifestation of ideals and desires takes place, the
unconditioned and forms an awareness. 'I am'
conditioned itself into the image and likeness of your
concept or idea, the 'I am' within you. The words you
speak have a strong influence on your feelings, moods,
personality, self-confidence and life experience. Earlier,
we pointed out how negative affirmations hypnotise us
into failure, disappointment, poverty, confusion and ill
health. So what is the solution? It is not very
complicated. Just apply the reverse process. Flood your
mind with power words or positive empowering
affirmations.
The affirmations that follow in the next pages declare
your strengths rather than your weaknesses. They focus
your mind on the positive instead of negative; affirm
what you are instead of what you are not, and what you
can do, instead of cannot do.

'I Am' has tremendous power, and what we manifest in
our life it is as a direct result of what we attach to the I
am.
The power of "I am" and when you say, think, feel I am,

you are the creator, this is the mystery, and the greatest secret many Sears, Profits, and Mystics have known throughout the ages.
I am is known as a lost word. The word 'I am' has never really been lost, but the real meaning has been lost and misinterpreted and misunderstood.

If you read and affirm and apply within you and understand you may just be surprised with the positive result within the first 30 days.

Your 'I am' will free you when you know what it is and how to use it. Be very careful what you attach to your 'I am', it has the power to limit you or elevate you and free you.
I am; what is I am?
It is who you really are, your true being, it is your real nature your real self and nobody else because no one else can say I am for you only you can say I am.
That is your real identity the presence of God, in you, the indwelling universe that is you, and whatever you attach to your I am with a conviction that you are and what you have will be made manifest.

You make your destiny and your own life by the same as what you attach to that I am, that is what you believe about yourself and how you feel about yourself.
If you surrender to fear by saying I am afraid, then you are destroying yourself every time if you entertain a pain of fear or jealousy or a sort of criticism.
Every time you speak I'm negatively you are manifesting adverse outcomes in your life, limiting yourself, breaking down yourself and you are making your body more sensitive to illnesses.

When you say:

I am loving, harmonious peaceful and strong you will
resurrect these qualities, and like God within you and
miracles will manifest in your life.
When people help you in the realisation of your dreams,
they are playing their part, and they are messengers
testifying to your beliefs and convictions.
You wrote the play another man and women execute the
parts to form into your concept of yourself.

Nobody can keep you away from your destiny.
Every time you allow the highest self to know and
believe and put your trust in God, you are lengthening
your life and improving your health and make it more
difficult for negative things to attack you.

Your I am not your consciousness is how you change
your world with whatever you attach to your I am you
become.

The top-secret: when you say I am you are now in the
presence of God within you, "I am" means pure being,
life awareness, self-originating spirit unconditioned
consciousness.

The power of these two words has been unknown to
most people because they are oblivious that when they
start the sentence with I am, they are proclaiming the
presence of God/Universe within them. I am called Om
in India, and many chant the word Om as a mantra.
It is essential to know that the meaning of the word Om
is before you use it.
'Mantra' in Sanskrit meaning: An instrument of thought.

I am, or the presence of God in your subconscious mind.
I am giving birth to the entire cosmos and all things
contained therein and is the only present power.

I am has to deal with the human heart or your subconscious mind. When you start to speak, I am that represents the infinite and change within you, which guide and direct you and reveals all the answers.
You can claim that God/Universe is guiding you in revealing to you the answer or solution to your problem. Accept the truth that the nature of infinite intelligence is to respond to you and you receive an actual answer.
Any person can fully affirm I am whole, perfect, strong, loving.
As you continue to believe all that you claim without the help or cooperation of anyone, you will start to manifest in your physical reality.
Express what you feel to be true remember whatever you attached to I am, you become.
 I am that I am; you are consciousness; you are the co-creator of your world and your reality. This is a mystery; this is the greatest secret that has been known for thousands of years. Your world is your consciousness objectified. Waste no time trying to change the outside; change within or the impressions and without and expression will take care of itself. When the truth of the statements downs upon you; you will know that you have found the lost words and the key to every door. A person should change their mind and understand that 'I am' has all the power, then it would be free indeed. And no longer have to rely upon intermediaries reporting some suppose it good that came out of the past.

◆ ◆ ◆

Every day and in every way I am getting richer and richer.
Every day and in every way, I am getting stronger and stronger.

◆ ◆ ◆

I dare you to say: Every day, and in every way, I am getting richer and richer. I dare to affirm ten times inwardly at any time the need arises. If you dare and will follow up the word with the mental image of yourself having all the riches you desire, your spirit substance will make your word manifest and show you the way to riches. All-day long you are manifesting with 'I am'. You can add to I am: rich or poor, sad or happy, sick or healthy. The universe can do for you only what you allow it to do through you. Make your daily assertion I am love, health, wisdom, truth, beauty, power for good, prosperity, success, unlimited ambulance. Never fail to affirm these things at least twice a day, 20 times is better.

The best and quickest way to manifest anything into a physical reality, correct our thinking and reprogram our subconscious mind is by the use of strong affirmations. To be repeated inwardly in silence, and anytime the need arises affirm the following; I am healthy, strong, young, powerful, loving, harmonious, loveable, successful, and happy. Just imagine you can free yourself from negative emotions and begin taking control of Your Life by Simply saying 'I am responsible'.
Whenever you start to feel angry or upset for any reason, the good news is that there is a direct relationship between the amount of responsibility you accept and the amount of control you feel.
The more you say I am responsible, the more of an internal focus of control you develop within yourself and the more powerful and confident you feel.
I'll erase my mind from all appearances of limitation to the contents of the one omnipotent power and affirm that I am the recipient of all its goodness and love.
 When do I say that Self is or Witness incarnate, do you comprehend what I am saying? Knowing it with your mind is not enough, the experience has to be there; is

that not strange: knowing and yet not knowing? Those who do not realise their Self, does their Self die with the body? No. even the 'Self' of ignorant people is immortal, but they fear death due to their ignorance. The one realises the purity of Self when he one encounters death. You are consciousness, pure existence, and this body is mortal. The Self is pure existence and a witness. In Self-awareness, there is immense joy, and in not knowing the Self there is a lot of pain and suffering. The Self is, super consciousness, the one who knows, pure existence, truth, ever-conscious. That bliss will come to you only with inward experience. Will be able to experience your pure consciousness with the daily practice of meditation. When would pain, suffering, jealousy, and hatred take leave of your mind? This will happen only when you understand and realise that the mind also is different from you. No doubt it is close to you, but still, it is not you.

The Buddha says that pain or suffering arises through desire or craving and that to be free of pain, we need to cut the bonds of desire. Entire cravings are the mind seeking salvation or fulfilment in external things and the future as a substitute for the joy of Being. In so far as 'I am' my mind, I am those cravings, those needs, wants, attachments, and aversions, and apart from them, there is no "I" except as a mere possibility, an unfulfilled potential, a seed that has not yet sprouted. In that state, even my desire to become free or enlightened is just another craving for fulfilment or completion in the future.

Witness how the mind labels it and how this labelling process, this continuous sitting in judgment, creates pain and unhappiness. Focus attention on the feeling inside you. Know that it is an emotional pain. Accept that it is there. Don't think about it - don't let the feeling turn into thinking. Don't judge or analyse. Don't make an identity for yourself out of it. Stay present in the now, be a watcher, an observer of your pain. Every emotional pain that you experience leaves behind a residue of pain that lives on in you. It merges with the pain from the past, which was already there, and becomes lodged in your mind and body. This, of course, includes the pain you suffered as a child, caused by the unconsciousness of the world into which you were born.

This accumulated pain is negative energy that occupies your body and mind, and it is caused by the blockage and interruption of natural energy flow that passes through our energy centres (chakras).

More on this in the following charters, but for now, I can tell you that this can easily be alleviated and permanently removed by regular mediation.

If you master to stay alert and present in the now and watch whatever you feel within, rather than be taken over by it, it affords an opportunity for the most powerful spiritual practice, and a rapid transmutation of all past pain becomes possible.

When you've understood the basic principle of being aware as the watcher of what happens inside you - and you "felt" it by experiencing it - you have at your disposal the most potent transformational tool. Be a witness. Remain detached.

You just be a watcher, a seer; be aloof from all this paraphernalia of the world and the body.

Only then can you enjoy, otherwise you will suffer as no scenario is ever going to remain unchanged.

Change is bound to happen as it is the very nature of the mind and this whole world.

An enlightened being would say: if it is birth, that is fine even if it is death that is also fine - as nothing can happen to the Self. The realised ones would say: What can death take away from me? – Nothing! All the dramas of this world are happening in front of me.

"I" am the witness, pure consciousness, indwelling being, the divine within. Let it happen whatever has to happen, Therefore why worry. "If you plan on being anything less than you are capable of being, you will probably be unhappy all the days of your life."
Abraham Maslow

Chapter 8 - SELF-LOVE

Most of my clients had a problem with self-love. They struggle to feel love for themselves and to feel lovable. To a degree, most people struggle with the same. All of them desire to elevate their feeling of deep self-love and to feel loved by others. The more people struggle with self-love, the less they can acknowledge the love given by others. A number of my clients have said: "I don't feel loved by my partner, wife, husband." It wasn't because their partners didn't give them affection and love, but because of their inability to receive love. Some clients even said, "I don't believe that anyone truly loves me if I don't love myself," "How could they?" "I am quite sceptical." A lot of people say; I can't trust anybody, I can't trust people, but what they're actually saying is; I am afraid that my two fundamental human needs will not be met. And that that I live in fear of being rejected, and I have a deep desire to feel loved. You need to learn to love yourself first and learn how to love yourself unconditionally, open your heart so you can overflow with love, and give it freely without expecting anything in return. Loving yourself isn't easy. It seems like the kind of thing that should come naturally, but research has shown that most people are filled with a reasonable amount of self-doubt and, as a result, their minds fill with self-deprecating thoughts from time to time. It's okay to struggle with self-love, but it's not okay not to give it a really solid try.

You deserve to love yourself because, no matter who you are, you are awesome, and "you are enough." So

start embracing your awesomeness and use the five tips below to start loving yourself now.
There's no time like the present to learn to love yourself!

1. Stop comparing yourself to others. The entire world encourages us to compare, to want what others have, to want to be like others. We loose enormously when we waste time judging others and ourselves. If you genuinely want to love yourself, you must stop your comparisons. Focus on you, what's great about who you are, how you are, what you have, and what you do. Look inwardly at your real self, the indwelling being, the infinite beauty, infinite love, consciousness. Don't waste any more time comparing yourself to those around you or on social media. It's the first -- and most important -- step to loving yourself now.
2. Focus on your achievements -- big and small. Too often, we focus on the things that went wrong (or could go wrong), and not on the things we did right, or envisage positive outcomes. We'll dwell forever on a conversation that went poorly but hardly think at all about a beautiful interaction we had with someone. Likewise, people are often more likely to focus on their failures than their achievements (as some sort of self-protection in order to avoid future failures). It's okay to acknowledge the things that didn't go swimmingly, but if you really want to love yourself, you have to spend most of your time thinking about what you did/said right and try to do more of it. And, remember, even the little things deserve a pat on the back.
3. Look past the mirror to your true self. It's all too common for people to define themselves by the way they look. Remember: you are more than what you look like. Yes, it cannot be denied that appearance is important and has some merit, but it is not everything. The way culture is set up, it's hard to remember that sometimes. Next time you look in the mirror and find

yourself filled with negative thoughts, remind yourself that you are more than what you see in that reflection. Every time you look at yourself in the mirror, say "I am enough," write this on every mirror in your home, on your phone as a screensaver, computer, everywhere where you could see it often and affirm as often as possible "I am enough." Your true worth is more than the way you look. Once you convince yourself of the truth in those words, it will become much easier to love your true self. You are pure consciousness, indwelling, the divine within.

4. View yourself from another perspective. We all have a tendency from time to time to get wrapped up in our own minds. Our thoughts and ideas take over, and we tend to forget that there are millions and millions of other opinions and ideas out there that could benefit us. The next time you find that you're giving yourself a hard time, take a step back and try to look at the situation -- and yourself -- objectively. You may soon realise that the way you were looking at yourself or the situation is not the way that others would. Taking a step back and looking at yourself with fresh eyes will help you to realise that you are worth more than you think -- and you are certainly deserving of your own love.

5. The attitude of gratitude. Make a list of all your remarkable traits. Feeling like you're not entirely up to par? Stop. Drop what you're doing. Grab a paper and a pen. And get to work. The activity might seem like a silly one, but seriously, taking some time to write about how great you are will help you to realise that, no matter how you might feel about yourself sometimes, you really are pretty amazing. Write ten things that you are grateful for? For example, "I am grateful for being alive, for my breath, for my eyesight. And if you find yourself struggling with this exercise, enlist the help of friends and family. Hearing their input about your awesomeness will make you realise that, hey, if all of those people can

love you, you can undoubtedly love yourself! Starting a Gratitude Jar is one of the most powerful things you can do to create positive exponential changes in your life. Focusing on what you have to be grateful for, forces you to not only become a more positive person - but to attract more positive situations into your life because they become self-fulfilling prophecies of the thoughts you're putting out into the universe. And when more and more amazing situations begin coming to you to feel grateful for - that's the point you realise your life changed into something incredible. Even Oprah put a gratitude jar on her favourite things list, so you know it's incredible. Gratitude jars provide a simple way to cultivate the habit of being mindful of the good things in your life. Each day, you write down one thing for which you're grateful and put it into the jar where they collect as a reminder of the good things in your world. Studies show that a sense of gratitude can improve the emotional and physical health of adults and children alike.

Here's how to make and gratitude jar:
- Start with an empty plastic or glass jar. A peanut butter or mayonnaise jar work well, but you can also go with something larger if you have it. Plastic or glass jar will work.
- Anything goes for decoration. You could practically use any craft item to decorate the jar. Some people colour the paper they apply. You could pick affirming words to cut from magazines and glue to the jar. You can even cover it with cut-out photos of your family. Have fun!
- Don't forget the lid. This is a great place for you to label the jar or really stake claim to it by putting your own name on it.
- Make the slips. Cut out blank squares of paper on which to write things for which you are grateful. You can also use a small notebook for this if the pages will

easily tear out and fold small enough to fit quite a few into the jar over the coming days, moths.

- Kick it off. Start the gratitude process by writing one thing for which you're grateful and putting your slip in the jar.
- Choose different things to be grateful for each day. The idea is to choose something different to be grateful for each day for a year. First seven days will be easy, after will be a bit more challenging. By persisting in finding one new thing to be grateful for, you are literally reprogramming your mind to be happier as you continuously look all day for one new thing to be grateful for that you haven't put in your gratitude jar previously.
- Add a slip to the jar each day. With the jar ready to go, pick a regular time to write the gratitude slips—maybe in the morning or at dinner or bedtime. As you add a slip each day, soon, the jar will fill with reminders of good things in your life. If you are having a bad day, take out, and read some of the gratitude slips and then find something new to add to the jar. Then on New Year's Day (or any other day 3, 6 or 12 months later), sit down and go through the gratitude jar, literally counting the blessings and resolving how to appreciate and celebrate them in the coming days.

You could have one Gratitude Jar separately, for your spouse and for each of your children, and follow the same process as above. Enjoy, and have fun!

Keeping a Gratitude Journal

The essential practice is straightforward. In many of the studies, people are instructed to record five things they experienced and felt for which they're grateful. The entries are supposed to be brief—just a single sentence —and they range from the mundane ("waking up this morning") to the sublime ("the generosity of friends")

Tips for reaping one of the most significant psychological rewards from your gratitude journal:

Don't just go through the motions. Research suggests that journaling is more effective if you first make the conscious decision to become happier and more grateful.

Motivation to become more joyous plays a role in the efficacy of journaling. Go for depth over breadth. Elaborating, in detail, about a particular thing for which you're grateful carries more benefits than a superficial list of many things.

Writing, I am grateful for my mother it's beautiful, but what would have a more profound impact would be if you think about and list seventy-eight thousand things your mother did for you to raise you all these years. Get personal. Focusing on people to whom you are grateful has more of an impact than focusing on things for which you are grateful.
Try subtraction, not just addition.
One effective way of stimulating gratitude is to reflect on what your life would be like without certain blessings, rather than just tallying up all those good things. Savour surprises.
Try to record events that were unexpected or surprising, as these tend to elicit stronger levels of gratitude — serendipitous moments.

Choose different things to be grateful for each day. The idea is to choose something different to be grateful for each day for three, six, or twelve months. The first seven days will be easy, and then it becomes a bit more challenging. By persisting in finding one new thing to be grateful for, you are literally reprogramming your mind to be happier as you continuously look all day for one

new thing to be grateful for that you haven't put in your gratitude journal previously.
I am grateful that you are reading my book!

◆ ◆ ◆

"Love yourself. Enough to take the actions required for your happiness. Enough to cut yourself loose from the drama-filled past. Enough to set a high standard for relationships. Enough to feed your mind and body in a healthy manner. Enough to forgive yourself. Enough to move on."
Steve Maraboli

Chapter 9- REMOVING NEGATIVE HABITS

Make a list of everything that is right with you. Take a good appreciative look at it. Go over it frequently. Even memorise it. By concentrating on your assets and qualities, you will develop the inner conviction that you are a worthy, competent and unique individual.
Whenever you do something right, be sure to remind yourself of it and even reward yourself for the action. In this way, you will build up a new habit pattern of concentration on what is right with you.
Focus on what's right about your life. Keep your mind off of what you don't want and on what you do want. Remember what we focus on we create more of!
As you apply the principles in this book, a successful NEW YOU will emerge.
You will be an individual of power, direction and planned action.
You will overcome the false beliefs that have been holding you back. You will be a friendly person who is never lonely.
You will be a self-reliant person who controls his or her own destiny. You will not need to judge yourself or others.
You will be a poised individual with empathy for others.
You will be open and receptive to new values, concepts and beliefs.
You will have radiant health and longer life.
You will have a new Spiritual Awareness.
You will learn to love yourself and others more intensely than you ever have before.

A bright picture isn't it? Sure it is because it is a view of YOU once you have learned and applied the principles contained within these pages.

This will take a commitment to action, but it will be one of the greatest adventures of your life. Once you have committed yourself to improve your life mentally, physically, spiritually and to build total self-confidence, you will never be the same again.

Use the following suggestions to condition yourself to substitute any harmful habit that you find detrimental to your wellbeing.

Step one: write down the following:
A.   What negative habit do you desire to replace?
B.   What positive habits or attitudes will you develop to replace them?
C.   What actions will you take to replace your negative habit?
D.   What is the most natural and most logical way to do this?

Step two:
A.   Visualise yourself as already having succeeded in changing your habit. See yourself enjoying the benefits of your new positive habits.
B.   Use a positive affirmation to go along with the visualisation.

Step three:
Observe your actions and note every time you fail to do what you promise. Remember, DO NOT condemn or scold yourself. Simply make a non-judgmental observation and allow yourself to make the necessary corrections.

Step four:
Keep a record for at least ninety days.
After you consciously choose your new positive habit pattern, these four steps will enable you to program it into your subconscious. It will then become an automatic response action.
If you have established negative responses to life situations, your automatic mechanism will cause you to respond the way you have conditioned yourself to FEEL and ACT.
It is advisable to monitor your responses or habit patterns by using the following three-step formula to evaluate and correct them.
1.   Remove anything in your life that is not working for your good, that feels heavy and doesn't align with your heart and soul.
2.   See what is working for you and continue to program that into your subconscious.
3.   Add new things you find desirable that are likely to work for you.

Use the above formula for the rest of your life, and you will find that you will gain self-confidence, and your life will be full of successful experiences.

Building self-confidence requires action; it is not something you can wish for, purchase, or borrow. There are things you can do every day to help build your self-confidence.
Here are a few suggestions:
- Practice positive thinking
- Be aware of your negative self-talk and replace with positive
- Visualise success and positive outcomes every day in the past tense
- Accept compliments and believe them
- Seek coaching through difficult times

- Identify your values & goals
- Be honest in expressing your strengths, talents, and skills
- Learn from constructive criticism
- Write down your accomplishments every day
- Give credit & praise yourself every day
- Take action on ideas you believe in
- Nourish your physical, mental and spiritual self every day
- Forgive yourself and those who have hurt you
- Make time for self-development every day
- For the next ninety consecutive days, commit to wake up early (one hour before normal waking-up time), meditate, read motivational self-help books, or listen to audiobook, podcasts, watch motivational videos, exercise, eat healthily, get a coach, or mentor during challenging times. Implement these positive rituals for at least ninety consecutive days until they become automatic positive habits, and your life will improve exponentially.

The truth is, you cannot change or control anyone but yourself. When you learn not to spend time worrying about changing others and work on changing yourself, you are on your way to higher self-confidence. Improving yourself can be as simple as wearing a different colour that cheers you up or as difficult as getting rid of a bad habit, such as smoking. Change may mean learning new behaviours or letting go of harmful or destructive relationships.

Decide what you want and how you would like to change. Write your ideas below, then do the following visualisation and affirmation exercise.

Find a piece of paper and write your ideas:

Now, affirm (state in positive terms) how this quality makes you feel about yourself.

Here is an example of a positive affirmation: "I am completely confident in all that I do. I do my best in everything I undertake. I feel good about myself, knowing that I am becoming more and more confident every day."

Write your affirmations on a piece of paper and read them over and over until you memorise them. The more you practice them, the more your mind will accept them, and the more it will become part of your life.

◆ ◆ ◆

"Whether you think you can or think you can't,
you are right."
Henry Ford

BE CAREFUL OF THE COMPANY YOU KEEP
Everyone whom you associate with affects your life. Make it a point to not only hold positive conversations but as much as possible to associate with only positive people. These are the people who will inspire, motivate, and help you to live a more creative life. Negative people drain your energy with their constant putdowns and complaints about how the world has mistreated them, how their husbands or wives don't understand them, how their bosses don't value them, and how terrible they feel. Whenever possible, release these "energy vampires" from your life and seek out people who are uplifting and positive.
Many people believe that a positive mental attitude is unrealistic. But this is not the case at all. Positive thinking is a way of looking at your own problems and those of humankind and trying to solve them through constructive action. The difference between the negative and positive thinker is rather like two people's reaction to half a glass of water. The negative person says that

the glass is half-empty, but the positive person knows that the glass is half full.

There is a third choice: What glass? There is no glass! There is only water, shapeless and formless. Soft but most potent. Fluid and flexible. Be like water.

A positive mental attitude allows you to build on your strengths, overcome your weaknesses. It helps you to realise that you were born to be great because within you is the power that you can use to make any dream a reality. It helps you to focus on the good things in life and allows you to give your dominant attention to what is right with you, other people, and the world. By seeing good around you, you generate a magnetism that attracts more good into your life. For, as we have noted like attracts like.

◆ ◆ ◆

But understand this: POSITIVE THINKING IS USELESS UNLESS IT PROMOTES POSITIVE ACTION.

◆ ◆ ◆

We have bought into the lies that we are not enough, that things are not available to us and that we should settle and accept our unhappiness, that happiness, love, success is not possible to us. The lie that because we are different, we don't deserve to have it all. We spent our lives hearing from others, "You are not good enough," "You are not; strong enough, clever enough, fast enough, pretty enough, young enough, old enough, thin enough," it is impossible for you. It is not available to you; you must settle and accept how you are and who you are.

We are bombarded by advertising companies, and on social media telling us to buy this, that or the other product. And that only if we look a certain way, wear

certain clothes, acquire particular objects, we are worthy, and we are good enough, and that one day we will be happy. We have bought into the lie that "One day when I (do this, that, obtain this, that or the other) I will be happy and fulfilled."
How many times have we felt empty after we have obtained something? One day when I……….. I will be happy! "Happiness is an inside job." Happiness cannot be acquired or arrived at; you can only decide to be happy, just choose every day, first thing in the morning to be happy. You cannot have or do happy; you can only BE happy.
Just decide!
Decide to be happy with the process and enjoy the journey, and you will feel more fulfilled once you reach the destination.

We bought into the social premise that who we are, our self-worth, our profound value is measured by our external achievements, diplomas, certificates, awards, how many material objects we have, and money in the bank.
But no amount of external achievements, material objects, or money can ever give us profound happiness and fulfilment that we desire.

The idea that one day when we buy a new car, get a new job, have a pay rise, have more money, open a business, buy a house, we will be happy. One day when I have X amount of money in my bank account, I will be happy. One day when I look a certain way, have several material objects, I will be happy.
When I get him/her and have a casual or serious relationship, I will be happy. One day when I get married, have a baby, I will be happy. One day when I have my children, house, car, money, I will be happy.

The idea of one day when I.........I will be happy has made most people so miserable that people are always striving for the next thing, hoping and praying that the next thing will make them happy. Perhaps when I get this next thing, I will be happy.

One day when I have £10,000 in my savings, I will be happy. They achieve the goal, still not happy. One day when I get £100,000 I will be happy and again not happy. One day when I get a £1 million, I will be happy. Surely now I will be happy, but No. Happiness has been eluding them most of their lives; because one cannot do happy or have happy, one can only be happy.

I am not saying you don't pursue money in life or material objects, on the contrary. I am saying, seek as much money as you believe you can manifest, £100 million, £1 Billion or more, but learn to be happy first and practice habits of feeling profoundly delighted and fulfilled from within, and be happy with the process of creating and manifesting. When you learn to be profoundly happy and fulfilled from within, you will learn to love the journey and learn that happiness is the way.

You have to ask yourself why you want to manifest hundreds of millions of billions? Is it because you'd like to hoard the money or to share it and contribute positively to humanity? Research has shown that people who manifest £100 million + easily and quickly are the people who have created products and services that contribute positively to humanity and these people also do a lot of philanthropy and they are the happiest and most fulfilled.

◆◆◆

"There is no way to happiness, Happiness is the way!"

Have an inward experience and a new you will emerge.

Chapter 10 - MENTAL HEALTH

◆ ◆ ◆

Mental health affects everyone at some point in their life, and it shouldn't be ignored. When we think about health, most of us only focus on our physical health. We do physical exercise, experiment with different diets, try to eat healthily, most go for a regular doctor check-up, but very few invest the same amount of time and attention on their mental health. Mental health is no different from your physical health and shouldn't be overlooked and ignored. The route cause of many physical health issues stems from the neglect of persons' mental health.

Mental health doesn't care if you are rich or poor, young or old, doesn't care about gender, sexual orientation, the colour of your skin, or if you are religious or not. We are all equal (we are all one) and belong to the same race, 'The Human Race," and we are all equally susceptible to mental health issues if left unchecked and unattended.

It affects people from all walks of life; children, teenagers, stay at home mums, teachers, bus drivers, athletes, artists, accountants, bankers, lawyers, doctors. No-one is immune to the mental health issues if neglected. Stress, depression or anxiety account for 44 percent of all work-related ill-health cases in Britain, and 57 percent of all working days lost due to ill health, according to the government's health and safety executive; Work-related stress depression or anxiety statistics in Great Britain published on 31st October 2018. The recent article of the Financial Times describes many cases of mental health issues that stem from stress and burnout at work and number of cases of suicide. The article named: "The trillion-dollar taboo": why it's time to stop ignoring mental health at work Research has shown that self-harm is the leading cause of death amongst 15-45-year-olds, all around the world.

What are you doing for your mental health, personally, at home with your family, at work, at school, or in your business as an employer? Is your employer providing any support or training for your mental health?

I asked all of my clients and the number of other people from all walks of life the same question: 'What are you doing for your mental health?' These are some of the answers that I received :
- Nothing, should I?
- I am not mental.
- I don't like this fluffy personal development stuff.
- Why? I don't have mental health issues.
- No! I wouldn't want to be stigmatised or discriminated against.
- Not at the moment, I wouldn't want my employees to feel that I am implying that there is something wrong with them.
- I think it is employs responsibility to do something on their own.
- I am unaware that there is any help offered in my workplace, and I don't feel comfortable talking about it.

Research has shown that the vast majority of people do very little for their mental health on a regular basis and usually only when there is a crisis.

Sometimes too little too late as many cases show when people end their own lives, and often their loved ones are unaware of any issues.

Recently, friend's boss committed suicide. Tom was only 42, a very successful trader and investor in the city of

London, earning more than £10 million per annum. He was married with a wife and three children, had beautiful homes all around the world, many other investments, cars, sailing boats. Tom was a very bright young man, loved by his family and friends, and on paper had a perfect life.
His family and friends were completely unaware that Tom had issues and are still in shock.

It appears that in Great Britain, mental health is a taboo topic, and people generally don't like to talk about it because of the fear of being stigmatised and discriminated against. Very little is made available for the employees in the corporations for the same reason. Research has shown that burnout in the workplace is the primary cause of the growing health issues.

I think it is a cultural thing, and many keep it bottled in, and self-medicate with drinking alcohol, consuming drugs, or eat a lot of food, amongst other things, to help them cope with emotional pain, past traumas, stress, anxiety, and depression.

When you speak to your friends and loved ones, the conversation typically goes like this; You: How are you? Friend: I am good, thank you. How are you? Then friend talks about their work, relationship, all the things that they've been doing such as; holiday, shopping, watching favourite show, football or other sports. Notice the question; how are you were never really answered. And you do the same, talk about having and doing. Even if you haven't seen a friend or family for a while and catching up, you would typically talk about having and doing, and seldom about feelings. You'd be surprised; people live under the same roof, and no-one truly knows each other. To truly know a person, next time, make an effort to really find out how the person is feeling and help them open up and feel vulnerable around you. You don't have to do anything or help fix them or their situation, only to listen. Almost always active listening is all the person needs to feel better.

By creating a safe environment for your friends or loved ones to really be heard, listened, and understood is the true sign of friendship and love.

Ideas for better mental health:
1. Watch your language and learn to be mindful of your automatic negative thoughts. Most of us have a negative inner voice. Negative mental rehearsal is habitual that was acquired years ago, and it often passes undetected under our conscious awareness.
You might think or say:
- I am too old.
- I am not good enough.
- I have a bad memory.
- I am not good at maths.
If you keep constantly saying any of the above or similar, that will be self-fulfilling. If you fight for your limitations, you get to keep them. Any sentence starting with I am not should be eradicated.
You have already learned about who you indeed are in the previous chapters and by saying 'I am not', you are putting limitations to unlimited possibilities of the universe shining through you. Your mind is always eavesdropping on your self-talk!
2. Positive peer group: How inspired, encouraged, challenged are you by your peer group? Excluding your family; people you choose to surround yourself with. If you are not elevated, inspired, energised, and challenged to grow and improve by your current peer group, choose new peers. Because this really affects your mind, body, and spirit.

3. Positive Diet for your Mind. Be careful what you feed your mind with every day.
You could be in solitude, choosing to read negative information, following news propaganda and fear mongers, negative videos, violent video games, and negative social media. Eradicate any harmful mind food and only feed with more positive and uplifting. Choose positive content for your mind daily that elevates and inspires you.
4. Push beyond your pain period. Mohamed Ali was asked: How many sit-ups do you do in your training? I only start counting when it starts hurting, he responded. People often give up as soon as it becomes difficult, and they start feeling some pain. You might have periods of pain in your relationship, in your job, business, in your health, and feel like giving up when the going gets tough. To grow and improve, you must push through the pain.
5. Sleep & Rest Good sleep can improve concentration, productivity, maximise athletic performance, creativity, improve the immune system. As you drift off to sleep, your body begins its night-shift work:
• Healing damaged cells
• Boosting your immune system
• Recovering from the day's activities
• Recharging your heart and cardiovascular system for the next day.
6. Learn new things: Research has shown that people who live over 80, 90, even over 100 years of age are lifelong learners. Increase your longevity and your brain neuroplasticity by constantly learning and practising new things. If you read a book and discover wisdom and methods that resonate with you, don't just read once, read it several times, study and practice. Same as learning how to play a musical instrument or a new language, you wouldn't just do it once and be good at it, would you?

7. Stress management: Exercise regularly, eat healthy food, daily positive habits and rituals are paramount for stress management and overall mental and physical health. Avoid or reduce alcohol and drug intake.

The first hour of the day and the last hour of the day is the most important to micromanage and implement the preplanned positive rituals daily such as; Meditation, visualisation, reflecting, affirmations, incantations, lofty questions, gratitude list, daily journal, reading self-help books, audiobooks, watch inspirational & educational videos.

Try to avoid digital devices an hour before bed and read books instead of using any device that emits blue light; phone, tablet, laptop.

Chapter 11-
TRANSFORMATION

◆◆◆

As you know by now, to understand who you truly are, you can't do it intellectually or conceptualise it; you have to experience it. You will begin to experience deeply who you truly are when you start to meditate daily and consistently, sitting in silence and solitude.

The process of inwardly experiencing who and what you indeed are, happens in 3 parts;

Part one: Accepting that you are more than the body and mind. You might read this book, understand that you need to do the deep internal work, and keep putting it off. Trust me, I know it could be challenging and scary, and definitely, it was for me and most of the people I worked with. At first, it was terrifying when I decided some 25 years ago to work on myself, I felt I needed every ounce of courage to begin, and I kept putting it off. Or had done the meditation and other positive rituals a couple of times and was frightened to go back. I can tell you now, It does require a lot of courage to start, because it is not familiar, and in order to have the deep experience required; you must not have any expectations on the outcome. Just need to trust it to surrender, to fall inwardly. Don't worry; you will not hurt yourself when you fall as you will do so in the deepest self-love, self-confidence, infinite creativity, and Infinite abundance.

Part two: This middle part could be messy, and you might feel that you are making mistakes, it is an unfamiliar territory after all. You have practiced meditation and other positive rituals for a few weeks, and have had a number of experiences where you had released some of the old stories, old pains, old traumas of your five-year-old self. Some of these experiences were very painful, and you probably cried a little or a lot, and it was messy and scary. During these moments, you might have been wondering if you are supposed to be feeling like this, in this unfamiliar territory. But it is normal to experience whatever comes up; there is no specific template that fits all; you have to experience your true self in your own unique and individual way. Some of my clients, including myself, began to have deepest experiences of release after only a few days and deep experience of self-love and self-confidence. You begin to be congruent and feel in the alignment of who you truly are, and you begin to do everything from this deep alignment with your soul. You listen to your heart more and become more confident to say no to things and people that don't align with your true self. As you remove a number of impediments, clouds, curtains, people, situations, and begin to experience on a deeper level the congruence of your indwelling highest power, you change energetic vibration and tune into the highest frequency of the universe. From this frequency, you begin to experience positive coincidences and serendipities all around you. You begin to meet new people that align with your true self. The kind of people who elevate you spiritually, mentally, emotionally, and physically in both personal and work life. You start saying yes only to things and people that align with you and are in congruence with your soul. And saying no to things and people that don't align without ever feeling guilty. Saying no to activities or rituals that have been detrimental to your mental and physical health such as consuming alcohol, drugs, unhealthy food, or other escapism activities such as 30 hours a week of social media or mind-numbing tv watching. You might have done those activities in the past because you had never experienced who you truly are and had a need to suppress or avoid any potential negative emotions. Now that you have experienced your true indwelling power, and how amazing you are, you live with your heart courageously open and release anything that is not in alignment with your highest self.

Part three: When you live from this profound place of who you truly are, everything begins to feel easy and effortless, because you have opened your heart and soul exponentially and live unapologetically as your deepest and truest self. You release the need to people please, and it truly becomes none of your business what they might be thinking or saying about you. You feel such a sense of freedom to be your true self, courageously claim your power, and shine your light the brightest from within, and without having the need to dim your light for anything or anyone. By doing so, the other people around you feel this unconsciously and feel the permission to start shining their lights brightly too. From this place, you begin to experience and create magic and miracles internally and externally. You experience deep self-love overflowing from within you, creative ideas pouring from within you effortlessly, You become a conduit for infinite universal intelligence, creativity, love, and abundance channeling through you effortlessly. You experience deep inner peace, bliss, confidence oozing, and stress becomes a thing of the past. Linear time becomes almost irrelevant to you, as you are in the permanent flow with the universe. When you are in this zone, you often lose all the scenes, creating for hours, you have so much energy, don't feel tired, and often forget to eat.

Now you are like nature co-creating with the universe easily and effortlessly. You feel so excited and thankful all the time to be alive and to be able to contribute to

yourself and humanity. You might have been a seeker for most of your life, reading books, going to courses, seminars, and implementing different strategies and techniques externally to arrive at this place of being your true self.
Now you feel that you have finally found yourself fully, and experience your true nature, your true power of who you are and who you have always been.
We have been taught to look externally for our true self, and that we need something or someone external as an intermediary for us to arrive at the experience of who we truly are.
We have been programmed since childhood to look on the outside for what we need, but when we experience our true power inwardly, we begin to realise that we don't need anything, that we are already full and complete.
For decades we have been hearing people saying that they want to change the world. And now we have the young generation and millennials, or generation z, (not sure what the correct label is), anyhow; human beings are saying that they want to make an impact.

Some people in our history have changed the world through activism, protests, riots, violence, revolution to a certain degree, and generally been protesting against something outside of themselves.
The people in history who have made a long-lasting positive impact on humanity were the people who were standing for something and not against.
These same people, like Mother Teresa, and Nelson Mandela worked on themselves internally for years and as a result, helped to heal humanity and change the world.

You can only change your life and change the world to the extent that you change and improve yourself inwardly.

Stop focusing your attention on what is wrong with the world, and with people around you, instead divert your entire focus on working on improving yourself inwardly for 90 days, one year, two years, or however long it takes, you will improve your life exponentially and as a result, change the world. If you are one of those people that is blaming your parents, the society, the government, your boss, the economy, your spouse, your children, or any other people for the quality of your life, for the quality of your relationships, your happiness, and fulfilment.

You will suffer, and your life will only improve when you divert your entire attention on working on improving yourself.

For your life experiences to change, first, you have to change. If you are experiencing any of these things in your life, it is because you have never truly worked on yourself.

Focus your attention inwardly and work on changing yourself and improving yourself.

I do 2 to 3 hours of deep work meditation every day, so I can tell you from my personal experience that it is the most important and most rewarding experience.

Butterfly and Caterpillar story

As you begin to practice meditation, other positive rituals, transform positively, start to live in congruence with your soul, and your highest calling. You will hear a lot of people around telling you that you shouldn't, they will try to give you advice based on their self-limiting beliefs.

It is like you were a caterpillar most of your life and you lived surrounded by other caterpillars, looking down at the ground, never knowing that you could transform into a beautiful butterfly and fly.

As you begin experiencing internal love, confidence, and happiness, other people around will try to convince you that you are wasting your time on this fluffy personal development stuff. Now that you are a butterfly and have had several fantastic flights (inward journeys, and positive transformation), you might be inclined to justify to the caterpillars in your life why you've decided to improve. You will try to explain that it's so amazing to fly like a butterfly and feel open and vulnerable, but the caterpillars will do anything and say anything to convince you that you are crazy and that butterflies don't exist. Because you feel incredible now, and care about people in your life, you will try to explain that everyone can transform into a beautiful butterfly, be profoundly happy and fulfilled.

They would want you to stay the same, do the detrimental activities with them, as you used to do before your transformation. They will tell you that you are no fun anymore; call you crazy. Tell you that you lost it. Call you names, insult you.

They will do anything to convince you that butterflies don't exist and that you should stop dreaming and come down and look at the ground all day with the rest of the caterpillars.
Now that you have grown in confidence and have had many beautiful transformations, just give love form the distance and don't try to explain or convince them. Don't waste your time or energy.

On your journey, you will encounter people who would try to knock you down, with comments, opinions, and subjective views. It's because they'd rather knock you down for improving and growing than focusing on their inward feelings of unworthiness and lack of self-love. Don't despair, as these are the people who need love the most, and they wish to experience what you have.

Focus on your inward journey, self-development, and people who are ready to fly will ask you how. Not everyone you care about, including close friends and family, are prepared to transform into a beautiful butterfly and will remain caterpillars for the rest of their life.
Your energy and focus should be on flying, growing, developing, and expanding your network of other butterflies.

Other butterflies could come in the form of a mentor, coach, people (butterflies) who had several flights, books, videos, audios, workshops, and seminars. Your aim should be to expand your support network of likeminded people who could help you on your journey and elevate further.
For some people, it could be heard to fly and stay on the beautiful journey of growth and transformation. They might quit and go back to their old stories and old habits.

Have an inward experience and a new you will emerge.

Being a caterpillar for most of their life is very familiar, and in some cases, people go back to walking on the ground with wings tacked in, even though they have transformed into a butterfly. Flying, amongst other amazing butterflies, it's unfamiliar and could be daunting for some people. So after several flights, they might go back to the old habits and old stories of being a caterpillar and barely surviving instead of thriving.

People have been telling me for years that I am very deep, and what I talk about is very profound. Back in 1994, when I first learned about this timeless, universal knowledge that has been written about for thousands of years, I wanted to share with anyone I could. I was so excited that I wanted to talk to anyone who would listen but often experienced dirty looks, sarcastic jokes, or insults.
I soon learned that I couldn't talk to caterpillars about exciting flights of butterflies and of the possibility to heal their pain and transform positively beyond their wildest dreams. I understood that I should divert my entire attention on transforming myself inwardly, and as a result, I could contribute to humanity more.

Some of my closest friends have been in my life for 20 years, and I have observed their own growth and transformation, and I learned not to give any advice if not asked. I've learned that everyone is on their own inward journey of self-discovery, develop and transform at their own pace.
Many have told me that I've had a positive impact on them, and it was often through indirect help.
I have tried most of my adult life to shine my light brightly, and courageously opened my heart, and in doing so, unconsciously giving permission to people to do the same.

I've had many setbacks on my journey and have had many experiences where I've dimmed my light to fit in. And even though I transformed into a butterfly many years ago, and often after having several fantastic flights, I had gone back to the ground, tucked my wings and walked with the caterpillars. I did this to fit in, worried that I might lose friends I've known for years, but often at the significant detriment to myself, and I was unhappy and unfulfilled.

I had released few people that were not in congruence with my soul, strengthened the bond and the relationship with the ones that remained and made several new friends that are happy to transform into a beautiful butterfly and fly with me.

The day I decided not to dim my light for anyone, to be my true self, shine my light brightly, unapologetically, open my heart fully and vulnerably, this was the day I began to feel profound love, happiness and fulfilment.

People say: I like her/his energy, they are looking in the mirror when they say that. They are feeling the same positive energy and attributes beyond mind and body that resides in them.

They were complimenting the invisible, nonphysical stuff that makes us who we truly are. When we feel another person with these amazing nonphysical qualities elevated, we can't help but have a deep connection with them, as it's a reflection and a reminder of who we indeed are.

◆ ◆ ◆

If you are seeking profound love, happiness and fulfilment:

I invite you to be your true self, shine your light brightly, unapologetically, open your heart fully, vulnerably and fly like a beautiful butterfly that you are.

◆ ◆ ◆

I think by now you pretty much know who you indeed are and what you are capable of, and I hope you have practiced meditation and other positive rituals every day since you've started reading this book and have had experiential understanding. I sincerely hope you did and will continue to meditate and practice other positive daily rituals because the contents of this book can only be understood by doing deep internal work and having an experience, and not understood intellectually.

Chapter 12 - LOVE

"The best and most beautiful things in this world cannot
be seen or even heard,
but must be felt with the heart."

All the love you will ever need is already inside of you.
When you learn to love yourself, you will never again
need someone else to validate you to feel loved.
Interestingly, at the same time you realise this, you will
attract an abundance of people who love you. You
cannot honestly give love abundantly to someone else
until you have learned how to love yourself. And you
cannot attract a lot of what you do not know how to
give. All of the answers to everything you want are
already inside of you.

Another way to think of this for those seeking their
'significant other' relationship match—Until you love
yourself, how could you attract someone else who does?
The idea is dysfunctional in and of itself, which is why it
leads to dysfunctional relationships. If you need
someone else to validate you, of course, you will attract
someone who is not confident in who they are as well.
And for as long as two people in a relationship are not
confident in themselves and can not love themselves,
they will never be able to give love to the other truly.
Instead, they will continuously be seeking proof that the
other loves them, and finding plenty of reasons to
believe that they are not loved. It leads to dysfunction,
conflict, unhappiness, blame, unfulfilment, and,
ultimately, a break-up.
It's why most relationships and marriages end.

The answers are all found within one's self, that's the good news!

◆ ◆ ◆

"We experience profound love when we allow our most vulnerable and true selves to be seen and known, and when we honour the spiritual connection that grows from that offering with trust, respect, compassion, kindness and affection."

◆ ◆ ◆

The purpose of romantic relationships is giving. Giving is the key ingredient? How can I give that suits you? How would you like to receive? Don't just give in a way that you think it's appropriate, ask your lover, your spouse how they would like to receive.

Magical relationships and genuine relationship bliss don't just happen; you have to work at it every day and look for ways to grow and improve positively.

At least once a week, I sit down with my wife and ask the following questions; Do you feel understood? Do you feel loved and appreciated? What can I do more off to celebrate our love and our relationship? I choose to focus on the positive attributes of the person, particularly in my marriage. I always think about what it is that made me fall in love with my wife in the first place. And all the things that make me love my wife more each day. And how I can elevate my love and appreciation for her after six years of being together. What is it that I value, and that I admire about my wife and I focus on that, in order to cultivate truly magical relationship.

When you fall in love with someone, you fall in love with how they are complete. You don't want to change them, shift it around, you don't want to change that, you don't wish that they look different, you don't wish that they are something else. You fall in love with who and how they are. And you keep that in mind, remind yourself every day, and look for more ways to love them and appreciate them.

There are many definitions of love, yet each one is inadequate. Love can be found in the dictionary somewhere between 'like' and 'lust.' And perhaps that's where it belongs!

To understand what love is, we have to understand what love is not.

Love is not hating, violence, ambition, or competition. It is not infatuation.

Infatuation focuses only on external traits and is merely a form of conquest, which fills a personal need that is invariably followed by disappointment.

For example, a woman marries a man because he is handsome, then says that all he thinks about is his looks. She marries him because he is intelligent, then feels stupid and accuses him of knowing it all. She marries him because he is steady and sensible, then finds him annoying and dull. She married him for his money, then is unhappy because all he thinks about is business. She marries him because he is sexy, then objects when he is sexually attracted to other women. And on and on it goes!

These examples are not love, merely infatuation. The same examples could be used for any gender. Love is not sex. You can have sex without love and love without sex. But when sex and love are combined, the result is a beautiful, spiritual experience, one unmatched by any other.

What, then, is love?

Love is the attracting, uniting, harmonising force of the universe.

Love is the desire to support a person in being all that they can be. It's helping the other person to grow emotionally, mentally, and spiritually. Most of all, love is allowing another person the complete freedom to be himself or herself and accepting that person without trying to change them.

To love means to love, period! It doesn't imply conditions such as "I will love you if…….." "I will love you as long as..." or "I will love you when..." Love that implies conditions is nothing more than emotional blackmail.
I am talking about; to love without any conditions.

In order or preserve love, one must not attempt to change the other. It happens much too often, and it's one of the major contributing factors to break-up and divorce.
Love, romance, and excitement are all possible when you permit your partner to express her or his individuality. When a relationship is not stifled by unreasonable demands and expectations, it will grow closer and stronger. The more independent you feel, the more you will value your partner. True love depends on true freedom. Only those who feel free to be themselves can afford to love without reservation.
Learn to love everything that happens to you because your experiences give you a chance to grow in the consciousness of love. Say to yourself many times a day, "I am growing in the consciousness of love." As you do, it will enrich your life in marvellous ways.

Many people go through life, hating, criticising, and condemning others for their lack of love. These are negative people. They have a talent for putting others down with joking sarcasm and making them feel so inadequate and useless that they either hold back, withdraw or plain give up.
Negative people withhold love, recognition, and complement because they must always say what is on their minds, regardless of how destructive it is. They

justify their verbal hostility as "constructive criticism," an "honest relationship," or even "objective appraisal." Their greatest talent lies in the ability to find and identify the weaknesses in others instead of their strengths.

It is common knowledge that, when plants are praised and spoken to positively, they thrive and grow, but when they are condemned and rejected, they become stunted or even die. If you have this effect on your plants, think of the impact you have on another human being!

Similar results are observed in the rice experiment (three rice jars) was invented about ten years ago by Dr. Masaru Emoto, an "alternative-science" researcher who believes in the literal power of thoughts and emotions.

I have conducted this experiment myself on the three identical jars with rice in 2014 for 30 days, and can tell you first hand that it confirms the following;

1. If we express negative thoughts and emotions towards the jar of rice, it has a negative effect.
2. If we ignore the jar of rice, it has a negative effect.

The rice experiment for 30 days.		
Jar 1. I hate you. Idiot. Retard.	Jar 2. Nothing written. Ignore and don't touch for 30 days.	Jar 3. I love you. You are amazing. You are the best.

3. If we express positive thoughts and emotions towards the jar of rice, it has a positive effect.

You can find out more about Dr. Masaru Emoto's rice experiment on the internet, but I do recommend that you try it at home for yourself. It is a lot of fun, and you get to experience a great lesson. You could do the same experiment with your children, and this experiment alone could teach them a lot about humility, compassion, kindness, and love.

If this is what happened to the rice after 30 days, think of the effect you have on another human being if you praise them and express love and gratitude twice a day.

Praising

Imagine praising your loved one, your spouse, your children several times per day, and listing all their positive attributes and what you are grateful for. What if you ONLY ever praise your children from birth and always watch your language and never insult them or say anything negative. Do you think your children would be very confident and loving adults? Most definitely! There is a lot of science backing this up!

Insulting

Now imagine the negative effect it has on a human being if you insult them several times per day for days, months or even years, if you insult your child, your significant other, your family, your friends, how about your boss?

How about if you have been insulting your child since birth (unintentionally) because it is the norm, everyone is doing it. I hear it all the time "you are a bad boy/girl," "you are such an idiot," "you are so stupid," "you are not good at this/that," "are you retarded?" During the insult, you also scream and shout at them at your little innocent three-year-old child who is so desperate for their parent's love, praise, and comfort so they can feel safe, loved, and loveable. Would this child end up being confident, a loving, caring, compassionate adult with high self-esteem? Highly unlikely! You would probably have to spend a fortune on therapy to try to help them improve their confidence and self-esteem.

Ignoring

Most people don't think about this. Still, surprisingly, when we ignore another human being, your loved one, family, children, significant other, and ignoring for a prolonged period, has a tremendously detrimental impact on this person and the relationship.
When we don't make any effort to positively nurture the relationship, spend quality time together, and give them your undivided attention. Staring at your phone during the interaction with people doesn't count as undivided attention. On the contrary, people don't like it and feel insulted and ignored. By ignoring the person you are saying; you don't matter to me; you are not important.
I know that in today's society, almost everyone is on their phone all the time and that "phubbing" has become a regular occurrence in many social encounters. Just because a lot of people do it, doesn't mean that when you are phubbing, you are not saying I don't care about you, you are irrelevant to me and are not hurting the feelings of your friends, your spouse, your family or your children. If you think you are not insulting other people when you are phubbing, try doing it at work to your boss in the middle of an important meeting; see what happens. If one person in a group is using their phone, that usually opens the door for others, who may start to think it's socially acceptable just because they keep seeing other people do it. After all, why would so many people be doing it if it wasn't okay? Wouldn't someone call them out on it?
Research has found that people were less satisfied with their romantic relationships, the more their partner was a phubber.

Ignoring any person that you are trying to cultivate a profound, meaningful relationship with is not alright, and it has a detrimental effect on the person and the relationship. Many conflicts in relationships begin when people ignore each other.

Instead, give a quality of undivided attention (quantity is not as crucial as quality), by doing so you are saying to the person; I love you, you matter, you are important to me. It could only be ten minutes of undivided attention to ask questions and listen and indeed find out how the person is.

Love is how we help others to be successful.
It expresses itself in the ability to make others feel important, alive, and capable of self-improvement.
By giving others recognition and assurance, and pointing out their positive traits, we can stimulate them to make the best possible use of their unlimited potential.
One of the greatest gifts we can give to other people is to open their eyes and heart to their greatness, to the possibility they never realised existed. It's what "loving thy neighbour" is all about.

But, helping others is not a one-way street. By offering encouragement and pointing out people's strengths, we are helping ourselves as well. Not only does this satisfy our own need for loving; therefore, each positive action generates an even more positive response and increases our total self-confidence.
I love everything I do. I am passionate about helping people, coaching clients, and I love writing this book for you!

Chapter 13 - IDEAL PARTNER

Most of us are conditioned to want a perfect or ideal partner.
We each seek out a specific set of qualities and attributes that are uniquely meaningful to us alone.
I want the perfect partner; tall, dark, and handsome.
I want the ideal partner, a lady on the street, and a freak in bed. I want x,y, and z.......!
Most of us want the partner to get something and focus on who they need to be instead of focusing on giving and who we need to become to attract and keep this partner.
Everyone wants a perfect partner, and few are willing to work on becoming a perfect one.

Attracting an ideal partner is about working on yourself first to attract what you perceive as perfect and ideal. If you are single and you have a desire to attract a deep, meaningful relationship try the following ideas;

Take out a pen and paper and start writing.
Describe in detail, who is your ideal partner?
Have fun with this:
What do they look like describe facial features, colour of the hair, and their eyes? The shape of their eyes, body, height?
After you have described in detail their physical appearance and their features, describe their personality, attributes, and what kind of partner are you looking for?
Are you looking for somebody understanding, compassionate, kind, loving, caring, and supportive?

How would you like to be treated by this partner? What would you be doing, what would you be talking about? Will this partner be giving you the kind of attention that you require? What kind of attention? What kind of love would you be looking forward to receiving from this partner?
Where would you be living with this partner?
Where would you be going on holiday? What would be your ideal date?
What would you be doing? How many times per week? Describe everything in detail for all of the above and anything else you could think of. You have probably written several pages on the A4 paper describing in detail your ideal partner.

Now, on the following pages describe who you would need to become to meet and keep this partner to develop a sincere, meaningful, lasting, loving, and happy relationship. People often envisage an ideal partner and want to meet somebody extraordinary, but they never consider that to achieve this kind of partner, they have to work on themselves first. And to get this kind of partner, keep, and maintain a deep, meaningful, happy, and lasting relationship, they have to work on themselves, growing and improving continuously so they can give and contribute.

People go into relationships for all the wrong reasons, and most of the time, this kind of relationship fails, ends up in separation, divorce, or lasts for a very short period.

To meet your ideal partner, to keep, and to develop a deep, meaningful, lasting, loving relationship, full of love and happiness even beyond the honeymoon period, you have to go in the relationship to give and contribute 100% of your ability.

Anyone looking for this kind of relationship has to go in only to give and contribute.

If you're going into a relationship to take and contribute only very little, no relationship will ever succeed, you will soon be found out, and the relationship will fail.

Any relationship for that matter, friendship, business, coworker relationship will not succeed if you are going in with the intent only to take, and not contribute much. The quality of the relationship will deteriorate and eventually fail.

To be able to give and contribute in any relationship, you need to work on yourself first — particularly your inner self and work on your internal improvement and transformation.

Fill yourself with your inner wisdom from your infinite intelligence, with self-love, self-confidence, compassion, kindness, and then you will have plenty to give and contribute.

But if you go into the relationship empty and not willing to learn and grow, you won't have much to contribute, and eventually, the relationship will deteriorate and fail.

Think about it; how would you feel if someone comes into the relationship with you and they are continually taking, taking!?

How would you feel about it, and how long will you tolerate that kind of behaviour?

You would feel that it has not been reciprocated. After the infatuation or the honeymoon period, you will realise that this is not the right person to create a deep, meaningful, lasting, loving relationship with, and the relationship will inevitably end.

When we go into any relationship to give and contribute unconditionally just for the sake of giving, both the recipient and we feel happy and fulfilled.

Once you find the special someone who is compatible and you feel that they're the right person to start developing a deep, meaningful relationship with, you should give and contribute from your heart one hundred percent of what you are capable of. Yes, but you don't know my story…….. You don't know how many times I had my heartbroken….. I don't trust people.
 I've heard it all before from my clients, friends, and family, and in fact, I used to say the same thing. I used to identify with the story of the experiences I had in the past.

I'd say: You don't know my story…. I suffered so much; my ex did a terrible thing to me; (eleven years ago). She gave me several STI's, and after hiring a private detective, I found out that I am not a biological father to our two-year-old son, and that she had been having an affair for over five years.
I had a nervous breakdown, when I found out, and went around as a victim telling my story to anyone who would listen, I was an absolute mess.
I felt so much pain; in fact, it felt like my heart was broken in half. I was moping around for a few weeks feeling sorry for myself until I remembered what I learned years ago, and began to implement.
My life began to improve, and I started to feel much better after four weeks of performing several positive rituals daily.
I started meditating for two hours a day, doing deep internal work, and feeling the pain dissolve. I began to remind myself who and what I truly am.
I was journaling every day and disidentifying with my story. It was only a story, not who I am. It was only experienced, not my entire life, and what my ex-girlfriend did; she did from the place of her limited awareness. I used to identify as; she did this to me, my

life, my girlfriend, and once I began to disidentify with it, I began to feel much better.

It was very hard at first to write and say; this and that happened, and at that time didn't occur to me, that it happened outside of me, which I have no control over, it's done.
I cannot travel back in time and fix it. And my emotions, how I feel about what had happened, I am feeling inside of me, and I do have full control over how I feel.
Once I began to separate the real 'I' with the story and the experience and started to accept that what had happened is outside of me and that it did not occur to me, I began to feel much better.
I began to claim my power back, instead of feeling like a victim, and my life improved exponentially.

I reminded myself that when I did feel deep overflowing love, during the relationship with my ex-girlfriend, it wasn't because of her. It was because of me. It was because of who and what I truly am, and that infinite love resides inside of me. At my core, I am the endless love , and we all are.
I reminded myself that I don't need anything or anyone outside of me to feel deep love overflowing from within me, all I had to do was deep internal work of exploring the pain in my body in order to release it and dissolve it, while I was opening my heart more profoundly than ever before.
As I practiced these positive rituals, I also practiced forgiveness, and in this way, I claimed my full power back. We only feel powerless if we believe the myth that other people's actions could control how we feel.

Ideas and recommendations found in this book will only work if you implement them and work on yourself inwardly.

Have an inward experience and a new you will emerge.

Most of us are programmed to look externally and try to change the things and people on the outside so that we can feel great internally.

If we stop focusing our attention on what is wrong with the world, and with the people around us and divert our entire focus on working on improving ourselves inwardly for ninety days, one year, two years, or however long it takes, we will improve our lives exponentially and as a result, change the world.

Have an inward experience and a new you will emerge.

Chapter 14 - CAN WE BE HAPPY IN RELATIONSHIPS?

Yes, we can. We can truly thrive, be happy, and feel so much love and fulfilment in our relationships.
If you have the desire to improve your relationship, you will find ideas that you could consider implementing.

The ideas, rituals, and habits presented in this chapter, and this book have been fruitful for millions of people who have implemented them and for me.
But before I tell you what they are, let me discuss some of the challenges people face in their relationships and how to overcome them.

Most couples, after they have been in a serious, committed relationship or marriage, become complacent, think and feel that now that we are together, I can let myself go.
I don't have to do anything anymore, and I don't need to look after my mind, or body, physical appearance, mental and physical health, or spiritual growth.
I don't need to make any more effort to woo him or her, having a regular date night, finding things to do together spontaneously.

After a while, people take each other for granted and become strangers or roommates at best.
People and families live under the same roof as strangers, and no one truly knows much about the other; they are mostly disconnected and plugged in a virtual world through their smartphones or other digital devices.

We are told when we are children to work hard at school
to get good grades to get into university, so we can get a
good job, and continue to grow and improve at our job
or business to contribute more and do better.
Even after we get the job or open the business if we
wish to be successful, we continue to learn, go to
courses, seminars, workshops, read books, find a coach
or a mentor.
We continue to improve and grow so we could
contribute more, do better, and produce desired results.
If we don't continue to grow and improve every quarter,
six months, or every year and do better, we would
eventually lose that job or business.

Everyone I have worked with told me that; they desire to
be in and have a deep, meaningful relationship, full of
happiness, and profound love and fulfilment.

Why is it then that a lot of couples stop learning,
growing, and improving soon after they are in a serious,
committed relationship or marriage?
Logic will tell you that you have to continue to learn,
grow, and positively contribute if you desire happy and
successful relationships, full of love, joy, fulfilment, and
as I call it "The Relationship Bliss".
At the beginning of the relationship, we put our best foot
forward, really make an effort, which, if you think about
it, feels 'effortless,' and we do our best to woo our ideal,
compatible partner.
We make an effort to greet each other with a smile, kiss
(or in my case kisses and a long hug), and hug. We make
an effort to get up from the sofa and greet our partner at
the door as soon as we hear the keys, even if we are
watching football or our favourite TV show. Our newly
found (ideal partner) is our priority, and everything we
do comes from our hearts.

We are effortlessly; courteous, kind, loving, caring, compassionate, understanding, and supportive.

We feel that we are falling in love; our heart is so open and feels deeply happy to feel vulnerable. We might think that the other person is responsible for the way we feel, but the other person was just a catalyst.

These feelings of effortless profound love, overflowing from within us, have always been there, but to feel this kind of love all the time, first, we need to debunk a few myths and misconceptions.

Myth one: The honeymoon period only lasts for the first few months of the relationship.

What if I told you that millions of couples all around the world are head over heels in love with one another. And continue to be so every day for years? They continue to be so deeply in love even after 10, 20,30, 40, or even 50 years of relationship or marriage. They live in a relationship full of joy, fulfilment, and the feeling of profound and effortless, unconditional love. How do they do it?

There is no simple answer, but in this book, you will find ideas and principles that have worked for me, in my relationship with my wife, and equally for countless other couples all around the world.

Magical relationships and genuine relationship bliss don't just happen; you have to work at it every day and look for ways to grow, improve, and positively contribute.

Myth two: After the so-called (honeymoon period) people say; I am just too busy, I don't have the time or the energy to do what is required to achieve a fantastic relationship.

I provide coaching services to many clients, and other relationship coaches and therapists, and even they believed in many myths when they came to see me.

I bring to their attention that; you are not too busy to spend twenty hours a week scrolling aimlessly on social media and twenty hours a week watching your favourite shows or football. You do have energy when you come home from work to do so many trivial and unproductive things.

We have been brainwashed that the so-called honeymoon period lasts on average a few months to a year, and has to end at some point and that relationships become difficult after this period.
But that is not so. To create and maintain the type of relationship that resembles a honeymoon period during the entire relationship, for 2, 5, 10, 20, 30, 40, even 50 years, you have to work at it every day and look for ways to grow, improve and contribute positively instead of wasting time on trivial things.

Myth three: He/she is my other half?
That is the myth derived from romantic books, movies, music, and art.
Who invented this idea that relationships are 50/50?
Perhaps from the saying, he/she is my other half.
Probably the fib people bought into that two halves fall in love to make one whole. That 'I,' my true self is somehow finite, broken, and only half.
The idea that another person has to come into our lives and fill in our 50% emptiness somehow.
Many bought into the idea; that someone out there had the capacity to fill the heart-shaped hole inside of them and to make them complete. No wonder the Cinderella story is so popular.
I believe that two individuals are already complete, whole beings, and not two halves who come together to share their life journey. Each individual is whole on their

unique, individual life journey with their personal goals, dreams, and desires striving to grow and improve.

Two compatible, whole individuals meet, fall in love, and besides having their unique individual journeys, they also have a joint journey, with mutual goals, dreams, and desires.

Deep, meaningful relationships are always 100/100. One hundred percent contribution and commitment to the best of their abilities from both people.

50/50 is a transaction.

It is; if I do something for you, I am expecting that you do something for me. Now there are strings attached in the relationship. Soon we will only contribute if we feel that we will get something in return.

In this way, the relationship is conducted like a business deal.

Nowadays, we have turned love into a business. It is like in a business deal. We have a customer mindset that we need to receive something in return for what we give.

I need to have a possession in return mindset. Love and possession are entirely different. When you truly love someone, you think; I love you, and I want you to be happy. True love focuses on contributing what's best for our partner and seeing them happy and fulfilled.

Possession and 50/50 relationship think; I want you to make me happy, you need to give me, do for me so I will feel satisfied and fulfilled.

Love is; I want the person's best interest, and I want them to feel happy. Possession is I want the person, and I want them to make me happy.

If both partners are contributing 100% without concern of being paid back, they will have a successful relationship.

If we want a successful relationship, then we have to choose love over possession. True love is never 50/50; it is always 100/100.

The lure of romance is sweet, and many of us are
longing to experience the kind of soulful, earth-shaking
unconditional love that would transform our lives.
To experience this, we have to go inwards; it is our own
responsibility and our own journey of internal
transformation.
But transformation is somewhat challenging and messy,
and it doesn't usually come courtesy of a perfect partner
who's there to fulfil our every need and make us happy
and satisfied. It is not your partner's responsibility to
make you happy.

Myth four: It is my partner's responsibility to make me
happy.
 Make me happy, made me feel this, that or the other.
No one can make you feel anything; your feelings are
inside of you. The figure of speech is incorrect in itself.
Instead of thinking or saying you made me if you wish
to express how you feel, start a sentence with 'I feel.'

You alone are responsible for making yourself feel
happy and feel better about yourself by doing deep
internal work. It is not your partner's responsibility, they
might be able to assist you and help you on your journey
when they are not working on themselves, but ultimately
the buck stops with you.

We have to keep reminding ourselves; happiness is an
inside job. Partners' purpose is not to fill our emptiness
or to fix us, but to support us, and share the peaks and
valleys of life journey with us. And they aren't here to
feed into our idealised images of perfection. Most of us
already know this. But it's easy to put our blinders on
than to think about these facts.

Myth five: As soon as you have children, romance begins to die.
This cannot be further from the truth. Your partner is your lover first and foremost, and always will be, and just because you had children, they don't suddenly stop being your lover. When you have children, it does become a bit more challenging to find the time and to feel romantic, but it is possible if you make it a priority. Make it a priority to woo your partner weekly, spend quality time alone, and give undivided attention. Instead of just watching Strictly Come Dancing on tv, desiring to learn, but waiting for your kids to grow up first, pay for few dance lessons with your partner immediately (if you can afford it) and do what you love. Life is to be lived now, in the present moment, and not sometimes in the future.
I am sure you could find a couple of spare hours a week, to romance your partner, away from watching your favourite shows, sports, or using social media.

Myth six: My spouse is responsible to make me happy.Whether we are in a relationship or single, a relationship is usually only as good as our own relationship with our number one: our very own self.
If we don't like ourselves much and are unhappy or are lacking self-love, self-confidence, no amount of love and positive contribution from our partner will help us. To be able to contribute one hundred percent to our partner and our relationship, we must strive to grow and improve ourselves daily and consistently.
Our primary focus should be to improve the self-love, self-confidence, self-happiness and the relationship with ourselves.
The more we work on ourselves internally, the more we'll have to contribute positively to our partner and our relationship. Focus on cultivating your own sense of self

instead of criticising your partner for what you think they might be missing.

Your primary focus should be to work on improving yourself daily and consistently. We often tend to fixate on our partner's shortcomings when there is a part of us we haven't yet developed. Get real with your number one, if there's something you might need to work on to make yourself happy. And instead of fixing your partner, work on developing your own brilliance and mastery. Mistake that a lot of people make, and it's believed by many in our society. It's acting as if their romantic partner is the solution to their problems. The person who is supposed to automatically make you happy, and sprinkle magical fairy dust all over your life. This is an inevitable setup for disappointment. In truth, you don't need to share all the same interests, enjoy doing everything together, or even be best friends to have a successful and fulfilling relationship. When you centre your entire existence around the person you love, you miss out on so much: the beauty of your friendships, the activities you love to do regardless of whether or not your partner joins you, and your sense of self and independence.

The successful and joyful relationship is the one that helps you access the deepest, rawest and most real parts of yourself. The most fulfilling relationships aren't the ones that look good or always seem happy; they're the ones where you tap into your vulnerability and courage and engage in deep truth-telling.

The true intimacy is sharing the most venerable parts of yourself with your partner and trusting them to create a space for you, to the best of their ability, and without judgment. True intimacy requires that level of safety, which can sometimes be scary to ask for or venture into. Putting everything on the table with the utmost respect for yourself and your partner is what helps build greater trust and love while strengthening your bond.

Have an inward experience and a new you will emerge.

When we can accept that our partners are not here to complete us, we give ourselves a fair shot at the happiness we desire. That's because relaxing our attitudes around love and relationships naturally brings us back to what we are truly capable of, which is beyond our wildest expectations. It helps us see that wholeness is achievable not through perfection, but through changing our priorities so that we can embrace our imperfections (and that of our partner), connect to what we most value, and welcome profound love, intimacy, and relationship bliss.

So many people end up in relationships because they're convenient or because they don't want to be alone. You know that you're better than that, so get clarity on your priorities and what you want in a relationship and partner, how you're willing to change and improve to get this kind of partner and relationship.

This isn't about making a supermarket shopping list of the qualities you desire (like pretty eyes and a sense of humour); although that's a great start. It's more important to focus on your belief systems and whether or not your relationship choices are aligned with what you actually care about.

Do you continually fall for partners because they meet the requirements of your superficial, societally approved checklist? Are you paying attention to your deeper values and needs?

Often, you don't figure out what you need until you go through a relationship or two (or more), and this is OK. And please remember that just because a relationship ends doesn't mean that it wasn't successful or didn't fulfil a meaningful purpose, especially if it helped bring you closer to who you indeed are.

For me, every relationship that ended was a blessing, I learned so much about myself, and about what I truly want and need, and the universe conspired to help me meet my amazing wife, Nadia. Because of the past blessings and all the relationships that ended, I've learned how to give more, contribute better, communicate my needs and desires appropriately and develop deep, meaningful relationship full of joy and profound love and fulfilment.

Chapter 15 - OVERCOMING DIFFICULTIES IN A RELATIONSHIP

Myth seven: Being miserable in the relationship and arguing all the time, it's normal.
It is a general misconception that just because a lot of people are doing it, that is normal to argue in the relationship and to be unhappy. I have worked with many clients who had problems in their relationships, and the general premise is that it is normal to fight and argue all the time.
I worked with many relationship coaches and therapists, and even they thought the same at first when they came to see me. Many people will tell you that it is normal to be unhappy and argue all the time. And they might have an opinion that there is no solution. They might teach you techniques and strategies in how not to argue as often etc.

Some might tell you that: "Arguing is healthy because you get to communicate your frustrations and needs to your partner. Arguing does not have to be malicious or cruel — you can have loving and compassionate conflict. " Arguing or having conflicts is unnecessary, and nothing normal.
In my experience, arguing, fighting, and bickering every single day is not normal or healthy and should not be accepted or tolerated.
Many so-called experts and many books out there talk about how people are arguing and that it is normal and

acceptable in a healthy relationship - but I have to disagree strongly.

The techniques and strategies presented and taught by many so-called relationship experts, and the books available on the subject, advocate that it's normal and acceptable to fight, and argue in a healthy relationship and that it's not how often or how you fight, but you have to fight fair.
They present various strategies and steps on how to fight fair. I completely disagree with these views.
There is nothing healthy about fighting in any relationship and should not be accepted or tolerated.

I don't want to have a relationship where I am unhappy, and we argue all the time!
I want to be thriving, be profoundly happy, and fulfilled. I want to have an effortless relationship with my wife. I want to have a relationship where I fall in love with my wife deeper and deeper every single day. I want to have a honeymoon period for the rest of my life every single day.

Today I love my wife more than yesterday, and she feels the same, and we both express this every day.
The kind of relationship where we are both thriving. The sort of relationship where we have such a strong bond and feel loved, appreciated, respected, and understood.
A relationship where we truly feel comfortable to open our hearts deeply and fully and feel courageous to experience vulnerability all the time.
I pinch myself every day and ask myself; how could I be so lucky, and I express gratitude to my wife daily, and she does the same. We communicate this every day and have feedback.

This is the kind of relationship we have for the last six years and am confident that we will have for the rest of our lives.

When I tell my clients that they have to work on their relationship, it might feel challenging at first, but like with any new habit, after a while, it becomes effortless. You know all the right things to do and contribute daily from your heart, and it becomes effortless. The only way to create deep, meaningful relationships, full of deep love, fulfilment, and genuine relationship bliss, is by contributing positively daily and consistently.

If you are arguing a lot in your relationship, the chances are that you have a lot of unresolved, undigested emotions buried deep inside, causing you an upset and discomfort.
At the beginning of the relationship, your heart was so open (that's what happens when we fall in love), and each day you feel more comfortable to open your heart fully and be profoundly vulnerable.
You love your partner very much, but after a while, you begin to argue. When you fight, you might feel insulted or personally attacked, so you retaliate, you begin to close your heart, and mind more, each time you fight.

The fight starts to resemble a boxing match, each of you is throwing jabs and hooks, ducking and diving. And the more you fight, the more you close your heart and mind and condition yourself to be alert of a potential fight erupting at any moment.
You love your partner but feel very frustrated and somewhat hopeless, wish that you stop fighting so much and go back to how you used to be at the beginning of the relationship.

You want to feel your heart fully open and be profoundly vulnerable. That is your natural state, where you feel effortlessly and confidently yourself.
Without fully understanding this, and perhaps unconsciously, you know that you wish to feel the same again, and now you hold your partner responsible for taking this feeling of profound openness and a deep sense of love away.

You argue, don't talk to each other, make-up, have make-up sex (it feels great because your heart begins to open again), until the next fight, and you close your heart again. The reason that a lot of people get somewhat addicted to make-up sex, because it helps them to open their hearts fully, even if it's just for the moment, as at the beginning of the relationship.

Some people unconsciously become addicted to fighting and falling out because they are expecting the make-up sex and opening of their hearts entirely, even it is for just a few moments. And the cycle of opening your heart and closing continues.

Each time you fight; it may increase in intensity, you might shout at your partner louder, or insult your partner more because you don't feel that you are being understood. You don't feel that your feelings are validated, and you know that you don't want to feel like this again. Each partner feels that their feelings are not understood and validated, and they hold the other responsible for making them feel the way they do. Both wish to have their hearts open fully, experience deep love, and be profoundly vulnerable all the time and have the same experience as at the beginning of the relationship.
The more you fight, the more your heart becomes closed and harder to open, you start developing some physical

pains in your chest, stomach, neck, shoulders, or lower back. You begin to resent your partner, and as some clients told me: my wife hates me, she even said so. I don't feel any love from her; all I get is shouting, insults, and abuse.
I want to be happy, and for things to go back the way they were, they tell me. I can't take it anymore; I can't stand the fighting anymore, girlfriends/wive's tell me.
I feel so depleted, and I don't have the energy for anything. I am tired all the time, and I feel like throwing in the towel.

I want my boyfriend/husband to change and make me happy again. He used to be so lovely, he used to make me laugh all the time, and we had a great relationship. I don't know what went wrong, but I feel that if you teach me the techniques to implement so I can change my boyfriend/husband, so he can make me happy again.

You shouldn't be focusing on and wanting your boyfriend/girlfriend to change, you should only be focusing on improving yourself, and opening your own heart fully.

I explain to my clients why we fight in the first place, and what is the root cause. When they understand it and implement the techniques for ninety days, their relationship and their life improve exponentially.

Understanding that; what every human being wants and needs is the experience of the profoundly open heart and to feel vulnerable. You've heard countless times people say; I am scared to let anyone in because I am afraid they are going to break my heart. You also heard people say how amazing it is, at the beginning of the relationship, during the so-called honeymoon period.

At the beginning of the relationship, your heart was fully opened, and you felt free to feel vulnerable, you were on cloud nine, it felt amazing. I agree; it does feel amazing, probably the best experience and feeling ever.

The misconception here is that you think your new partner was solely responsible for opening your heart and making you feel so amazing, and when they break up with you, they are the ones responsible for breaking your heart.
Because you think and unconsciously believe this, you go and look for a new partner to help you open your heart and make you feel amazing again.
But no, they are not responsible; they might be the catalyst for the way you feel, but your feelings reside inside of you.

No one or anything outside of you can be responsible for the way you feel.
It is the feeling of our hearts being so genuinely open, and the feeling of absolute vulnerability that we all crave, often unconsciously.

We have bought into the idea that bickering, arguing, and fighting is normal in a healthy relationship.
A lot of people are doing it, so it must be normal.
We believe that insulting, screaming, shooting at our partner is normal in a healthy relationship.
Especially when they do or say something we don't like; its normal to insult them.
We believe that our partner triggers our negative emotions, and they are pushing our buttons on purpose.
We believe that our partner is responsible for our negative emotions and what comes out of our mouth when we insult them. He/she made us lose our temper.

If he hasn't done what he did, or if she hasn't said what she said, I wouldn't have to shout, insult, and argue with my partner.
When we express anger, frustration, hatred, and bitterness, at our partner, we say; they made me, it's their fault.

We think and feel like a victim and that it's not our fault when negative emotions and insults come out of us when directed at our partner freely and frequently.
But what comes out of us, its what was already inside; it is not our partners fault. Our partner should not have to feel like walking on eggshells and that at any moment, we will erupt in verbal abuse.

We are responsible for working on ourselves daily and consistently to remove any negative (old and unresolved) emotions that have probably been there (since childhood) before we met our partner.

We are responsible for learning and practicing daily rituals of opening our hearts fully and courageously feel vulnerable all the time. When we feel like this, we experience the deepest self-love, self-confidence, profound happiness, and fulfilment.

Chapter 16 - MAGICAL RELATIONSHIP

Try these ideas and recommendations below and in this book for ninety days constantly and watch how your life and relationship improve beyond your wildest dreams. Remember that the relationship you have with yourself sets the tone of the relationship you have with everyone else. If you want to work and improve your relationship, always start by working on improving yourself first.

Creating a magical relationship cannot survive on its own. It requires that both people work daily and contribute positively. It requires the care and nurturing of two adults, giving and contributing to each other in a way that creates a mutually beneficial bond, trust, love, respect, admiration, and appreciation. To create this kind of relationship, magical, sincere, and loving, there needs to be a daily positive contribution:

Communication, Listening, Honesty, Trust.
Instead of doing some of the trivial activities, like looking at your phone, or watching your favourite show, try to schedule at least 30 min each day (longer if required) for a deep, meaningful conversation. Without regular and daily communication, your relationship will not survive, especially if you have unresolved issues, unexpressed thoughts, and feelings. The more you communicate, the closer you will be, and the stronger the bond and love you will develop. Listening is perhaps more important than talking, try to find out what is going on in your partner's life, how they feel, what are they thinking, what they find challenging, how you

could help. Take turns in listening and let the other talk for as long as they need uninterrupted.

Best not to give any advice, just listen and let your partner get things off their chest. Before you begin, ask if they require any advice at the end of the conversation, or they'd just need you to listen. In most cases they will need you to listen without interrupting.

Good listening requires practice and patience. Honest communication and good listening allows the person to be vulnerable and creates the strongest bond, trust and love for each other.

Be open and undefended, and willing to be vulnerable. As a result, you will be approachable and receptive to feedback without being overly sensitive about any topic. Their openness also enables you to be forthright in expressing feelings, thoughts, dreams and desires. Honesty builds trust between people.

Dishonesty confuses the other person, destroying their trust along with their sense of reality.

Nothing has a more destructive impact on a close relationship between two people than dishonesty and deception. When a couple understands each other, they become aware of the commonalities that exist between them and also recognise and appreciate the differences. When both partners are empathic and are capable of communicating with feelings and with respect for the other person's wants, attitudes, and values, each partner feels understood and validated.

The willingness to work through difficulties and disagreements.

Throwing in the towel, even if you don't walk out the door, is not the path to happiness. You must face the discomfort that comes with differing opinions and ideas. Many difficulties and disagreements commence when we are not able to listen objectively. When a partner is expressing how they feel and we listen subjectively, we will feel personally attacked and we probably retaliate and say something hurtful to the other.

The other has the right to have different opinions, thoughts and feelings and express those without being judged or insulted.

We all have the need to feel safe in the relationship to express freely our opinions, thoughts and feelings. If something is bothering you, and before the difficulties escalate, say the following to your partner: I would like to have 10 minutes of your time to express how I feel, uninterrupted for the benefit of our relationship. If the other can't do or doesn't feel to do it immediately, schedule the time later that day. At the beginning of the 10 minutes (longer if required) meeting say the following: 'I would appreciate it if you could do me a favour and just listen for ten minutes (or longer) without interruption, you can make comments after I have finished. I have a need to express how I feel and get things off my chest for the benefit of our relationship. Only start the sentence with "I feel," and never "You make me."

For example, Girlfriend/Wife is upset because she feels boyfriend/husband doesn't give her enough attention and watches sports/football/favourite shows and says the following: When you watch TV for hours I feel sad, I feel that I am not receiving enough attention, I feel upset, I feel neglected, I feel ignored.

Write your own examples and begin with 'I feel' and never 'you made me.' When we have a need to express how we feel, we want to be heard and understood; if we start every sentence with you make me, you made me, the other will feel attacked and will not have heard or understood anything we were trying to express.

I feel upset. I feel unappreciated. I feel sad; when I made an effort to cook for us and made a lovely dinner, you were two hours late because you decided to go to a pub with your friends.

Refrain from sending insulting, angry text messages or screaming and shouting at your partner when they come home.
Express how you feel in person only, and always start the sentence with I feel.
Note; giving someone your peace of mind is not the same as expressing how you feel. The goal is to express how we feel and not to hurt the other. Verbal abuse often hurts more and leaves scars for a long time. Practice communicating respectfully and compassionately, and from a place of love. Expressing how you feel appropriately as per above strengthens the relationship.

Greet your partner with love. If you had a special greeting (hug, and a kiss) at the beginning of the relationship, continue with the same or improve on it even after years of being together. Don't take your partner for granted, or become lazy and complacent. Many clients tell me that after they've been in a relationship for a while, they greet their partner by remaining seated on the sofa, watching tv or looking at their phone, and without genuinely connecting, ask; how was your day? Often there is no kiss or hug when they are greeting their partner, sometimes peck on the cheek, they tell me.
It's unacceptable in any relationship. When we welcome our partner, they should feel that we are thrilled to see them, they should feel loved and appreciated. At the beginning of the relationship, the first few months, you're head over heels in love, and you are always putting your best foot forward. You are focusing on what's fantastic about your partner, that's your entire mindset, your attitude, energy, and you are always concentrating on being courteous and finding ways to show gratitude, appreciation, love, and support.

A sense of humour, and some fun. Just as we need to breathe to survive, your love needs fun to flourish. Giving your relationship what it needs to thrive is a truly loving gesture. You can't spend all your free time "working" on your relationship—don't make it a hobby. Discuss what you like to do, where you'd like to go, and how you both like to have fun. Then go and do it. Spontaneous fun with your significant other breaths fresh air into your relationship and keeps the excitement going.

Look for spontaneous new things to do with your partner that you would both enjoy and make it a surprise once a week or once a month. It doesn't have to involve a great deal of expense, like a romantic getaway or romantic dinner at a Michelin starred restaurant; it could be a free activity, there are many free activities that you could do close to home. Thought and effort in organising counts more than the amount of money you spent on it.

A sense of humour can be a lifesaver in a relationship. The ability to laugh at one's self and at life's challenges allows a person to maintain a proper perspective while dealing with sensitive issues that arise within the couple. Couples who are playful and teasing often defuse potentially volatile situations with their humour. A good sense of humour definitely eases the tense moments in a relationship. Besides, it always feels good to have fun with someone!

Never stop dating. Many clients tell me that they don't go on regular dates, and if they do, they might end up arguing or keep looking at their phones and not engaging in a conversation. As a result, they avoid going on dates if it's just the two of them.

Going on regular dates, weekly or fortnightly, should be one of the priorities in a couple's life. Arguing and or looking at their phones can be easily eliminated once you implement everything you have learned in this book. Treat your partner as a priority and make sure that they know this. Dates are special occasions and the moments when you celebrate your love and your relationship. These are the moments when you could list five things you admire or appreciate in or about your partner. Try to go deep and express in detail what you appreciate about your lover. Spend a night in a hotel, away from kids, in your home town at least six times a year, or once a month if you could afford it.

Sharing life lessons. When you discover something about life, or you make a self-correcting move that is healthy for you, and your relationship, let your partner know. You'll be surprised by the positive response. If you have read a positive self help book, watched a video, listened to an audio, read an article, and something resonated with you, share with your partner, your thoughts and feelings, and what you have learned. Try not to do it for the purpose of teaching or giving advice, share about what resonated with you, what inspired you, and why, and let your partner freely decide if they'd like to implement these new principles and ideas in their personal life.

Emotional support, and compliments. If you don't feel that your partner likes and respects you, there will not be a strong connection. You have to lift each other up and let each other know the depth of your caring. Make an effort to praise each other for the smallest things. Make it a fun game to think of new things that you could praise your partner for each day. Most people in a magical relationship daily express how they feel about their partner. My wife and I express how we feel about each other. Not just; I love you; we also express and list each day, several things we appreciate in our partner and all the things for which we are grateful.

Saying; I love you, Thank you for your cooking, cleaning, taking out the rubbish, its nice but has no depth, and our human need for each of us is that our partner sees us and appreciates us for who we are and how we are.

We feel so deeply loved, appreciated, respected and supported when we are told; Thank you for being so amazing, I appreciate your kindness, I appreciate your support, I admire your strength and your resilience. I'm proud of you. I appreciate that you make me want to be a better person. I love the person I am when I'm with you; you inspire me. I am grateful to have you in my life; I'll always have your back.

Thanking your partner only when they have done something for us (cook dinner, taken out the rubbish, bought us a gift, helped us with something) is not enough.

Love should be unconditional and saying; Thank you for being so amazing confirms to your partner that they don't have to do anything for you in order for you to love them unconditionally and appreciate them. You are acknowledging how amazing they are just for being, for existing in this physical presence, and just for being alive.

Praising each other and giving emotional support has to be worked on to become a daily ritual and a positive habit. We are conditioned to complain, blame, nag, and focus on the negative, to focus on what's wrong and what's missing.

The good news is that these negative habits and rituals are learned and browed from the people who don't have a clue about how to have a thriving magical relationship. If you are having difficulties in this area, learn new positive rituals and habits, and praise each other using the earlier examples or write your own.

When you start listing them, you will be surprised how many things you admire and appreciate about your significant other.

In my own relationship, since the day we fell in love over six years ago; my wife Nadia and I say at least one or all of the following to each other every day: Thank you for being so amazing, I appreciate you, I am so grateful for having you in my life, I appreciate that you make me want to be a better person, I love the person I am when I'm with you. I am proud of you. Also, we list and express several other attributes that we admire and appreciate in each other at least once a week.

We also give positive feedback about things that we like and would appreciate more of.

Be a cheerleader for your significant other and contribute with love, praise, kindliness, compassion, support, and understanding, and this alone will create a thriving magical relationship and true relationship bliss.

Love, intimacy, romance, and sex. These are the cornerstones of a thriving magical relationship. Being great roommates just won't cut it. There has to be the innate desire to be together, to grow and improve together, to elevate each other as a couple.

You may think the spark has gone, but there are too many ways to rekindle it. All you have to do is try and look for new ideas in how you can give and contribute more positively in love, intimacy, romance, and sex. Don't become complacent and take your partner for granted.

Continue learning about new and better ways of how you could contribute positively to love and intimacy and create a truly magical relationship.

You should be easily affectionate and responsive on many levels: physically, emotionally, and verbally. You should be personal, acknowledging, and outwardly demonstrative of feelings of warmth and tenderness.

Yous should enjoy closeness in being sexual and are uninhibited in freely giving and accepting affection and pleasure during lovemaking.

Next time you see a sixty-something-year-old couple who have been married for over 30 years, so in love that they cannot keep their hands off of each other, you will know exactly why and what they have been doing daily to have a such a magical relationship.

Sharing goals and dreams that resonate with both of you. Partners should feel congenial toward and supportive of one another's overall goals in life. They are sensitive to the other's wants, desires and feelings, and place them on an equal basis with their own. Ideal partners treat each other with respect and sensitivity. They do not try to control each other with threatening or manipulative behaviour. They are respectful of one another's distinct personal boundaries while at the same time, being close physically and emotionally.
Each individual is working on their personal goals, and they are happy in the process as well as when they achieve them. Besides personal goals, make sure you have mutual goals, and that always have something to look forward to and that you are pursuing it as a couple. Support and encourage each other in your individual goals and often talk about your mutual goals.

Compassion, acceptance, and forgiveness. These will show you the way through a difficult time. If you are together for a while, there will be losses, challenges, outside of your control, and some things that you can't fix. Weathering the storms together is a big part of what relationships are all about. These are the times when we need to look at the situation objectively, show emotional resilience, and give emotional support. Both partners should be empathic, capable of communicating with kindness, and with respect for the other person's wants, needs, and values, each partner feels understood and validated.

Whatever difficulties you are going through always try to communicate with compassion and kindness, as explained above.

Work through difficulties and disagreements. Understand that everyone is entitled to their own personal ideas, opinions, and beliefs. When challenges arise, try to understand your partner truly, ask open-ended questions, and listen. You will learn a lot about your partner in this way.

If something is bugging you, express how you feel with the sentence, I feel, and never you make me. Never blame or say things, so the other feels attacked or insulted. If something is bothering you ad your feel upset, express how you feel by starting a sentence with "I feel."

A mutual desire to step outside the box. The tried-and-tested is good, but the never-attempted-before may be better. Couples who are willing to learn together to improve their relationship, and share new experiences together, develop a stronger bond.

Each comes into the relationship with an old set of beliefs and perceptions based on their past experiences. Most of the time, difficulties in the current relationship are because of the past hurts, past negative experiences, learned negative beliefs and perceptions. If relationship bliss and the thriving magical relationship is your objective, and you are currently facing any difficulties, be willing to learn new ways together as a couple, and think outside the box.

Being able to admit mistakes and to talk about them. We all screw up sometimes, part of being a

human that is growing and learning always. Learning to understand and let go of mistakes that you or your partner make will turn your life around and give you more time for joy. Communicate from a place of kindness and compassion and express how you feel with the sentence I feel. Also, practice active listening.
It requires that you fully concentrate, understand, respond, and then remember what is being said.
If you've made a mistake, admit it and talk about it. If your error was pointed out to you, accept it, and talk about it with kindness, compassion, and understanding and don't become defensive and insult or attack your partner; this will never work and will only create more significant conflict.
—When there wasn't enough milk left for tea/coffee when we hit traffic and missed the flight.
Try to express how you feel without having your partner feel attacked or insulted, even if they've made a mistake. Yes, they've made a mistake, and we might have the urge to tell them that they are wrong and we are right. You might be thinking, let me give them peace of my mind, by insulting them, this will teach them a lesson, right? Wrong! You will only make things worse and create more significant conflict. Both partners should strive to live a life of integrity so that there are no discrepancies between one's words and actions. It goes for all levels of communication, both verbal and non-verbal.

If you must choose between being kind or being right,
always choose kind,
and you will always be right
Dr Wayne Dyer

Discuss taboo topics to improve your relationship:

- Finance
- Job/business
- Love & Intimacy
- Giving and contributing,
- Learning
- Communication
- Home
- Family
- Goals, Values, Motivation
- Household chores
- Health & Sickness
- Confidentiality
- Fidelity
- Feelings & Emotions
- Friendship

Sometimes we feel like we know someone, but on the surface, we are only familiar with the day-to-day.

We are often talking, but we aren't really sharing, even if we are married and live under the same roof.

We get so wrapped up in the day-to-day that we are lucky to get to the 'How are you?'

But we very rarely get to the 'who are you?' Especially when you have known someone for a long time, we forget to ask how they have changed. We let the deeper questions fade away. It's how people become strangers, living under the same roof. They stop sharing and truly knowing each other.

It is important to share and not just talk, not at only the beginning of the relationship but throughout.

It is important to know your significant other profoundly and intimately.

Some couples have relationship meeting scheduled in their calendar once a week or once a month, during which they focus on really finding out how the other is feeling; not just how was your day?

Often people assume that the other has the same values, ideas, opinions, feelings, goals, and desires about life and what makes us human. Just because you love each other, live together, attend the religious ceremonies together. Support the same political party, share hobbies or favourite tv shows, movies, and music. Go on holiday together and have children, doesn't mean that you truly know each other unless you share deep intimate, thoughts, feelings, values, goals, and desires regularly and consistently.

In my relationship:
At the beginning of the relationship with my wife Nadia, probably about three months into it, we already knew that we were going to get married one day in the future. We had conversations about many so-called taboo topics, so we could develop a deep understanding of how the other thinks and feels about certain things.
We drafted a relationship agreement (you can find a template on the internet) and spent a weekend discussing how each thinks and feels about several topics.
Such as; finance, love, giving and contributing, sex, intimacy, learning, communication, home, family, goals, values, motivation, household chores, health, sickness, confidentiality, fidelity. What does it mean to be in a fully committed, devoted, and faithful relationship? We discussed in detail about trust, help, support, emotions, self-confidence, self-worth, self-love, self-esteem, and our thoughts and feelings.
We discussed in detail potential situations that may arise in our future life together, and how we agree to heddle each case, where the boundaries are, and that we agree not to cross them.

Also, we had a relationship manifesto in which we decided to amend from time to time and to add new things to benefit the relationship further.
As the relationship progresses and you learn new positive things that resonate with your both, and you add new positive things to your relationship manifesto to benefit your relationship further.
You are continually working and learning how to contribute positively to your relationship.
Six years later, in August 2019, we celebrated our second wedding anniversary, we are so happy and in love.
I can honestly say that we are in love more today than the first six months of our relationship, and have developed a truly magical relationship and daily experience profound relationship bliss.

Just as you need to breathe to survive, your love needs a breath of fresh air to flourish and requires constant growth and learning on how to contribute more as a couple to achieve a pure relationship bliss and a magical relationship. Giving your relationship what it needs to thrive is a truly loving gesture.

Before you give up on your relationship, before you give up on yourself, try and implement the ideas and recommendations listed above and throughout this book for ninety days consecutively.
I promise you that your life and your relationship will improve beyond your wildest dreams.
You have probably never done this before and never contributed selflessly and unconditionally so it might feel heard at the beginning.
But like with any new habit, consistency is the key.
All of my relationship coaching clients that come to see me commit to working on themselves, implementing the teachings from this book, and contributing selflessly and

unconditionally. After ninety days, they have grown and improved exponentially, feel profound love, happiness, fulfilment and their relationship has never been better.

Activity

Commit to working on yourself daily for the next ninety days and contributing to your partner selflessly and unconditionally in love, romance, communication, listening, sex, and helping them in opening their heart fully. For the next ninety days work daily on removing any impediments, opening your heart fully and give like never before.

Learn to be courageously vulnerable and contribute in opening your partner's heart so profoundly that they overflow with love, joy, confidence and fulfilment.

Chapter 17 - RELATIONSHIP WITH CHILDREN

How to nurture unconditional love and loving relationship with your children? Having fantastic relationships with our children might be the true measure of the quality of life for many of us.
Our interactions with other people has a tremendous impact on the quality of our lives and our happiness and fulfilment.
In this chapter, you will discover that creating a great relationship with your children requires a significant shift in beliefs and perceptions.

Number one question you have to answer is:
Where are my relationships situated, out there, or in here?
It might sound peculiar.
If you have children, you'd say; it's situated in my children.

Everything starts with the thought and emotions attached to the thought.
Everything that you have experienced in the past commenced with a thought. Everything that you will experience in the future will derive from the thought.
Even the present moment started with a thought.
What you think about and focus on expands and magnifies.
If you understand that what you think about expends than everything you have experienced in your physical

world was manifested from your thoughts and feelings
that you've had.
The answer to the question:
Where are the relationships situated?
The answer is "YOU," every relationship it's situated
within you and experienced subjectively through you,
inside of you.

If you are focusing on what is missing, what is wrong
with my child and you always think about negative
things; he/she said this to me, he/she hurt my feelings,
he/she did this and that, he/she didn't behave as what I
perceive appropriately.

My children did something unacceptable, I got so angry,
so in my mind, it is acceptable for me to insult them and
call them names; you are an idiot, are you retarded, how
could you be so stupid, you are bad boy/girl, or even
possibly smack them.

I heard this many times from my clients and other
parents; my children have been driving me crazy, so I
lost my temper, and I disciplined them, and I showed
them who the boss is.
You have to scream and shout at children and sometimes
smack them, otherwise they'll walk all over you, they'd
say.

Parents think that screaming, shouting, and insulting
their children, calling them names, sometimes physically
disciplining them, is acceptable, that this is normal, and
this how you raise your children.
My parents did it to me, and I turned out alright,
everyone around me had the same type of parents, so it
is healthy and acceptable, they'd say.
I don't know any other way.

Your parents were born in the '40s, 50's, or 60's, didn't know any better, and had limited access to all of the information that we today have.

Well, the good news is that there is another way, and Is it possible to raise your children without them developing individual insecurities and self-limiting beliefs.

Yes, and it is also possible to help them reprogram their subconscious mind and install the new positive empowering program.

Even if you have been saying negative things to your children for years, it is still possible to help them and improve their self-confidence and self-love.

Good news is that this generation of parents now have more books, more videos, and more experts, who do indeed know what they're talking about. How to correctly raise your children, so they could develop into healthy, confident, loving, caring and compassionate adults, and be truly happy and fulfilled.

The scientists show that most of our decisions, actions, emotions, and behaviour depend on the 95% of brain activity that is beyond our conscious awareness, which means that 95 – 99% of our life comes from the programming in our subconscious mind. Also known as the habitual mind.

Research has shown that baby starts to learn and gets affected in the mother's womb, halfway through the pregnancy by the environment and by what they've been subjected to by their mother and father.

By the time baby is born, it has already learned many things in the mother's womb, as well as they possess many programs running in their minds such as bodily functions, instincts, feelings, and emotions.

Scientists believe that most babies are born with 100% confidence and profound self-love and that during the first seven years of their lives. And that their subconscious mind is in a permanent state of learning (download) installing new programmes, and new habits that they will use for most of their lives even as adults. All of these programmes are installed in their subconscious mind, also called the habitual mind, where they would remain most of their lives unless they are changed and replaced. Most of the adults are unaware that this is the case, and that 95% to 99% of their life is run by these programmes situated in the subconscious mind, and that they can reprogram them if they choose.

How much of the child's 100% confidence remains (if any) later in life depends on the amount of negative programming they've been subjected to as children.

It is a known fact that every newborn baby knows how to swim, and will continue to do so until parents programme fear of water in their minds.

A child goes near the water and parents scream, danger, danger, don't go near the water, you could drown. And then spend thousands on swimming lessons when a child is five years old to teach a skill that a child knew all along.

For some children, learning how to swim takes a long time because of the fear of water installed by their parents. I know several adults who are afraid of water and still say; I can't swim.

Now, as a parent, you spend most of the time with your child during those first crucial years of their lives. And almost all of your child's habits, thoughts, ideas, self-limiting beliefs and fears have been learned from you, and you have been responsible for the installation of their negative habitual behaviours and actions in their habitual mind.

Be very careful what you say to your children and, most importantly, how you say it because their subconscious mind is listening and waiting for the programme download.
Your emotional tone plays a big part in what you say and how you say it.

Negative programming:
1. Your child misbehaves, and you might say; you are so bad, I wish I never had you, you are such a bad boy/girl.
2. Your child brakes something or accidentally spills your glass of wine a the dinner table - you say; You are such an idiot, how could you do that, you start screaming and shouting, insulting them further, calling them names, stupid, retard, perhaps even smack them.

In both the above scenarios, your child "DID" something terrible, and every time you say, you are such a bad boy/girl to your child, scream and shout when they "DO" something bad. You are teaching them and programming their subconscious mind that they are bad boys/girls when they "DO" something and that when they are told you are bad boy/girl, there is no love for them from their parents.
Furthermore, after the event child continues to rehearse, I AM SUCH A BAD BOY/GIRL for days, months, or even years, and that is the programme that will be running in their subconscious mind.
Opposite is also true that when they "DID" something good, you praise them, hug them, kiss them and you say; you are such a good boy/girl, I am so proud of you, and now their mind is being programmed; when I "DO" something good, I am a good boy/girl, and my parents love me.

Is this unconditional love we supposed to have and give to our children?

Not in the slightest, we are teaching our children that our love for them is conditional, and if they "DO" something good, we love them and if they "DO" something wrong with don't.

Children will learn that my self-worth is linked directly with; if I do good or bad, If I do good, my parents will love me, seek constant validation, even as adults, and will carry this mindset in other relationships. Children are having these programming running in their brain; I can never please my parents, I want to make my parents proud one day. No matter what I do, I am never good enough, and I will never be able to please my parents. Children will learn this in their habitual mind and struggle with self-love, self-worth, confidence, and relationships for most of their life.

And even as adults when they get married unless they've learned how to reprogram their outdated programme that parents installed when they were children.

If you have been talking to your children like this, even only a few times, the chances are that they've grown up to be very insecure adults full of insecurities, self-limiting beliefs, and you might have had to pay thousands of pounds each year for therapy. And if they didn't go to therapy chances are they are miserable and unfulfilled, unmotivated adults who didn't do or achieve much in life and never truly live to their full potential.

Unconditional love should be given to your child just for being born, for existing and not put any conditions such as; if you do good, I will love you.

Positive programming:

1. Your child misbehaves - you say, darling, I need to talk to you about what you just "DID," mommy

loves you very much, and you are terrific, but what you just "DID" is so bad and it is not acceptable. You talk to your child, explain what they did, why it is terrible, and why they shouldn't do it again. I know you've made a mistake and that sometimes good kids do bad things, and today you did a bad thing. You still have to rein them in and tell them off, but never say 'you are bad,' 'you are naughty,' 'you are disgusting,' 'you are an idiot.'

2. You always say; you did something terrible, but you're good. Most importantly, it's what your child hears and feels when you say that. They hear and feel; my mother loves me unconditionally, I am amazing, and I understand that I did something wrong. And if you can just dialogue with your child, differently without attacking their self-worth and their self-esteem, chances are they will be different kids. In this way, you are disciplining your child and teaching them right from wrong, what is good or bad, but notice how their self-esteem has remained in tack. Now a child thinks my mummy loves me unconditionally, but I mustn't do that again because mummy explained to me, and I understand.

Therapist Dr. Viktor Frankl said that a person's problems are intensified by the feeling and meaning attached to the past events that affect them.
The meaning you attach to the event will affect you, so your parents getting divorced, of course, that affects a child. And the child will often attach the meaning which is "I wasn't good enough" for them to stay together, they didn't love me enough, I didn't make them happy, I should have made them happy, I failed to make them happy, so I'm a failure.

"I AM NOT ENOUGH" is a new self-limiting belief attached and programmed in their subconscious mind now.
So it's always the meaning you connect to a past event, and you have a mental rehearsal coupled with strong negative emotions running as a programme continually in your habitual mind. And in most cases, if left unresolved or untreated for the rest of your life.

In the situation with divorced parents, you have to talk to your child and say: Darling mummy and daddy are no longer together, that wasn't your fault, it was daddy and mummy that we couldn't live together anymore.
You know how daddy is living in a different house now, but he loves you very much, as much as he ever did, and will always love you, and daddy is still going to see you. Mummy and Daddy not loving each other the way they did; it doesn't mean that we don't love you.

Often a child will think that it was their fault that mummy and daddy are divorced, and they might think; I am not enough because I couldn't even make my daddy stay. If I were good enough, my daddy would've stayed. I am not enough is their new mental rehearsal.
Now you have to do a lot of explaining to children, and as long as you talk to them and tell that is not their fault, (you might have to do this several times), and keep reminding them that mummy and daddy loves them very much, and it's not their fault, they will be alright.

In this situation, where parents of young children get divorced, it's essential to talk to the children, explain and praise them.
Because in this situation, they are even more fragile and susceptible to install a programme of negative self-limiting beliefs, which could be very detrimental for the rest of their lives.

Remember as a parent you are 20 or 30 years older than you child and you are still a work in progress, battling through your internal storm and your own self-limiting beliefs (probably learned from your parents), haven't learned everything yet that there is to learn, and you still make mistakes.
You are not the finished article by any means, how could you expect your child to be at age 3 or 5?

Just remember the above the next time you feel like losing your temper and insulting your child for finishing the last bit of milk, and you have none for your tea or accidentally breaking something.

I have seen this with some of my clients and in a lot of parents with teenage children:
Now the child is a teenager, and by now you have developed a bad temper, and a short fuse, everything your teen does, it's irritating you, and you often scream and shout at them. You are probably thinking; I am only shouting and insulting them because I love them, and I just want what's best for them.
You don't talk to them anymore, you don't ask questions and listen, to indeed find out how they are feeling, what issues they might be dealing with, what they are thinking?
By the time they are teens, in your mind, you have already labeled them as a bad child, and in your eyes, they will never be better, so you always feel frustrated, complain, and tell them often how disappointed you are.

To you, this is all a normal and acceptable way to talk to children. You talk to other parents with teenage children, and they confirm that they too have similar issues with their children and that they too often scream and shout at their children. And this reaffirms your belief that this is normal, its only way to talk to children, and the only way to educate your children.

Everyone is doing it, and everyone is having the same issues with their children. It is today's generation of children; they misbehave and don't listen or respect their parents or anyone. It is the attitude of today's teens; they don't respect anyone. Back in a day when we were children, we were so respectful; we were taught to respect our elders, you'd say. But not kids today.
My parents disciplined me in the same manner, and I turned out alright.
And on and on you go, with the reasons and excuses to justify your wrong education and behaviour as a parent towards your children since they were born.
You would say, and do anything to justify that it was ok to programme most of their insecurities, fears, self-limiting beliefs, and phobias in your child. And in most cases, you wouldn't accept any responsibility for doing so. It is time you evaluate how you speak to your children, and what you say if you truly desire to raise healthy and happy children full of self-confidence and self-love.

Many other fears, phobias, insecurities, and self-limiting beliefs are learned from parents from birth to age seven, and many people later in their adulthood struggle to improve and overcome those self-limiting beliefs and fears.

These fears and self-limiting beliefs can be so incapacitating that stop many people from ever achieving their true potential, or ever living truly happy and fulfilled life.
When you focus all of your attention on what is wrong, all the defects that someone else has. And all that is

missing, that will be the experience of your relationship with that person. In this case, your children.
You see, you cannot be another person physically; you cannot be your son, your daughter, that it's impossible. So all you have to experience other people with, is inwardly, through yourself.
You are experiencing other people and the relationship you have with them only inwardly with your mind, body, heart, soul, thoughts, emotions, and feelings.

You have to understand and say to yourself; the quality of my relationships is not in who other people are, how they are, what they do, or how they behave towards me. The quality of my relationship is determined mostly by how I choose to perceive them, and my actions and feelings towards them. How I perceive them is all that have to process the relationship with.
Once you understand that you are the determiner of the quality of your relationship, you will stop focusing on what is missing, what is wrong with the person, and what you don't like in the relationship.

If you continue to focus on what is missing and what you don't like to in a relationship, you will get more of the same.
Whatever your dominant thoughts and feelings are about the person and the relationship, you get more of the same.

So what you want to do is; see the person in a positive light, understand that this person is also on their own unique, individual journey of self-development, understanding, growth, insecurities, self-limiting beliefs, self-doubt and they are probably fighting some internal battle as well.

These people have their good days and their bad days
when they are struggling with specific issues, as most of
us are. But these people also have a tremendous amount
of love, compassion, kindness, support, understanding,
and isn't it this that attracted you to these people in the
first place?
Isn't it that all their positive attributes, all of their
goodness, kindness, love, compassion, that made you
become friends, you became lovers, boyfriends,
girlfriends, husband's and wives?

How do you perceive other people it's how you will
experience them in your life. So if you focus on all their
positive attributes and all their amazing traits, you will
get more of the same.
What we think about and focus on, expands, and we get
more of the same.
It is the law of the universe.
The universe doesn't understand positive or negative,
good or bad when we think about something, and we
attached the strong emotion to the thought, it gets
manifested almost instantly.

If we desire positive experiences in our lives and
positive relationships, we need to develop more of the
positive thinking and emotions. And positive focus, what
we like in the relationship and we will manifest positive
outcomes.

If we genuinely desire relationship bliss, we would only
focus on the positive outcomes, and have positive
thoughts and feelings about the future of the
relationship, and perceive each person in a positive light.

Now you start to be careful about what you think and
feel because if you want to stay in the relationship, you

will start focusing on the positive attributes of the person, because what we focus on expands.

If you have children, you certainly can't stop the relationship with your children.
We can't get rid of our children if we are having some difficulties in our relationship. Yes, our children can be better and do better, but so can you.

Imagine how much harder it would be for you to improve and overcome your fears and your challenges if someone is always telling you that you are not good enough. That you are not cut out for anything; don't even try because you will undoubtedly fail.
When we focus on the negative, on what could be better, we are projecting our own self-limiting beliefs and fears onto our children.
If you continue to focus on what's missing, and all the defects in your children, you will experience more of the same.
But if you focus on all the positive attributes about your children, how good they are, how great they are, how helpful they are around the house, how good they are at school. How hard they try at sports and at education, how well behaved they are, how much gratitude do you have for having them in your life, those things will be made manifest even more, and you are going to have more things to be grateful for, for your children.

Remember that you are not the finished article by any means, how can you expect your child to be at age five?

Focus on praising your children often, be a cheerleader, and practice gratitude with them daily.

Making a Gratitude Jar with Your Child, in the same way as explained in chapter eight.

Have an inward experience and a new you will emerge.

Starting a Gratitude Jar is one of the most powerful things you can do to create substantial positive changes within your life and the lives of your children.
Teaching a child to focus on what they are, and what they have to be grateful for, forces them to not only become a more positive person, but to attract more positive situations into their life, because they become self-fulfilling prophecies of the thoughts, and feelings they're putting out into the universe.
And when more and more amazing situations begin coming to you to feel grateful for, that's the point you realise your life changed into something incredible.
Even Oprah Winfrey puts a gratitude jar on her favourite things list, so you know it's fantastic.

Gratitude jars provide a simple way to cultivate the habit of being mindful of the good things in your life. Each day, you write down one thing for which you're grateful and put it into the jar where they collect as a reminder of the good things in your world.
Studies show that a sense of gratitude can improve the emotional and physical health of adults and children alike.

Few examples:
I am grateful for being alive, for my breath, for my eyesight, for my health. I am grateful for feeling happy, healthy, and confident. I am grateful for my mother, father, sister, and brother, etc. etc.
Teach your children to go inwardly and to be thankful for the 'being aspect' of who we are as human beings, more often than just doing and having.
Being grateful for being: alive, healthy, happy, joyful, blissful, confident, loving, lovable, and having inner peace. Instead of just saying, I am grateful for my toys, etc.

The process of starting a gratitude jar is the same as in chapter eight; the only difference is the decorating aspect. Tell your child that you have a fun arts and crafts project for them, use a plastic jar if possible, (glass jar could accidentally break), and let them decorate with confetti, photos, drawings, magazine cutouts, or photos of the family. Anything goes for decoration. Have fun!

CHAPTER 18 - MEDITATION

"As gold purified in a furnace loses its impurities and
achieves its own true nature, the mind gets rid of the
impurities of the attributes of delusion, attachment and
purity through meditation and attains Reality."
– Adi Shankara

We are taught how to move and behave in the outer
world, but never how to be still and examine what is
within ourselves. To go inwardly and experience who
we indeed are. When we learn to do this through
meditation, we attain the highest of all joys that can ever
be experienced by a human being. All the other
pleasures in the world are momentary, but the joy of
meditation is immense and everlasting. This is not an
exaggeration; it is a truth supported by the long line of
sages, both those who renounced the world and attained
truth, and those who continued living in the world yet
remained unaffected by it.
In the parallel field of neuroscience, several experiments
with Buddhist meditators have shown that people can
actually change their brain structure (regardless of their
age) by creating new neural pathways just by conscious
thinking. The same research also shows, by the way, that
people who meditate regularly have higher immunity
and lower blood pressure, among other health benefits.

So what are you waiting for? There is a technique to suit
every type of man or woman; you just have to try them
out and find what 'clicks' for you.

I have practised different types of meditations in the last 25 years, and I find that Sahaja Yoga Meditation/ Kundalini Meditation and mindfulness meditation works best for me.
Meditation helps me with having a heightened level of awareness, especially with my thoughts, feelings and behaviours.
Other then for the practice of meditation, there is no method to develop control over the totality of the mind truly.
The goal of meditation is to go beyond the mind and experience our essential nature—which is described as profound love, peace, happiness, and bliss.

An important part of mindfulness is an awareness of our thoughts and feelings as they happen from moment to moment. It's about allowing ourselves to feel the present moment profoundly and clearly. When we do that, it can positively change the way we see ourselves and our lives.
Becoming more aware of the present moment can help us enjoy the world around us more and understand ourselves better.
When we become more aware of the present moment, we begin to experience afresh things that we have been taking for granted. Mindfulness also allows us to become more aware of the stream of thoughts and feelings that we experience, and to observe how we can become entangled in that stream in ways that are not helpful.
It lets us stand back from our thoughts and start to see their patterns.
Gradually, we can train ourselves to notice when our thoughts are taking over and realise that thoughts are simply 'mental events' that do not have to control us.

What is Meditation?

Meditation is a precise technique for resting the mind and attaining a state of consciousness that is totally different from the normal waking state. It is the means for fathoming all the levels of ourselves and finally experiencing the centre of consciousness within.

Meditation is not a part of any religion; it is a science, which means that the process of meditation follows a particular order, has definite principles, and produces results that can be verified.
In meditation, the mind is clear, relaxed, and inwardly focused.
When you meditate, you are fully awake and alert, but your mind is not focused on the external world or the events taking place around you.
Meditation requires an inner state that is still and one-pointed so that the mind becomes silent. When the mind is silent and no longer distracts you, meditation deepens.
Meditation is a practical means for calming yourself, for letting go of your biases and seeing what is, openly and clearly. It is a way of training the mind so that you are not distracted and caught up in its endless churning.
Meditation teaches you to explore your inner dimensions systematically. It is a system of commitment, not a commandment.
You are committing to yourself, to your path, and to the goal of knowing yourself and who you indeed are. But at the same time, learning to be calm and still should not become a ceremony or religious ritual; it is a universal requirement of the human body.

Buddha was asked, "What have you gained from meditation?" He replied, "Nothing!" Then he continued, "However, let me tell you what I have lost: anger, anxiety, depression, insecurity, and fear of old age and death."

Awaking your innate power Kundalini Energy

This innate power found inside all of us is called
Kundalini.
It has been called many names, but they are speaking
about the same thing. Every spiritual tradition has its
name for Kundalini - Holy Spirit, Grace, Shekhinah,
Anima, Chi, Bodhicitta- and every saint and mystic has
known Her blessing.
Seekers on all paths need Her grace to succeed on their
journeys. For this reason, shamans, yogis, monks,
priests, nuns and aspirants of all types approach Her as
humble servants of the divine.
Kundalini awaits the great awakening, the most
profoundly important event in the long life of the soul, a
life that extends over countless cycles of physical birth
and death.
This was the name given to the evolutionary energy that
is in all things. It is the feminine power of the universe,
sometimes called Shakti (Sanskrit word for power).
It is the vital energy of the universe like the force in star
wars; it is in everything and surrounds all living things;
it is the essence of life. In yogic literature and tradition,
it is said that each one of us has it laying dormant within
us the seed of this energy which is said to be located at
our sacrum bone, at the lower base of the spine.
Kundalini is often used to refer to the power of the
Divine present in each person. She has two aspects. One
maintains the entire existence of our body, mind and
spirit. The other aspect, considered dormant, is the
power of Consciousness to know the Divine in its
infinitude as Self.
This potential power, innate to us all, can propel our
awareness from the paltry limitations of individual
existence, with all its wants and needs and deficiencies,
to Unity Consciousness.

Kundalini is a Sanskrit term from ancient India that identifies the arising of our innate energy and Consciousness which has been coiled at the base of the spine since birth and is the source of the life force (also known as pranic energy, chi, bio-energy) that everybody knows.
Yogic science suggests that this energy triggered the formation of the child in the womb, and then coils 3 ½ times at the base of the spine to hold the energy field in stasis until we die when it uncoils and returns to its source.

The awakened Kundalini can stir up everything. Some people feel distortions of time and space, profound stillness and peace, healings, habits or addictions dropping away, inspired creativity, and states of boundless ecstasy and love arising for no apparent reason.
This is just a partial list of what may be experienced. While initial experiences may focus on physical, emotional and mental purification and transformation, shifts in values, attitudes and behaviours will also occur and have a major positive impact on relationships.
Awakening can also occur through other various yogic practices and disciplines developed over thousands of years specifically for preparing the mind and body for this vast influx of power and aiding in the arousal of Kundalini.
Prayer, devotional practices, chanting, selflessly serving others; meditation, mantras, ritual dance, drumming, and many other sacred endeavours can awaken Divine Consciousness, Kundalini.

Kundalini awakening is regarded as the greatest prize on the spiritual quest; the blessed soul receiving this grace is on its way to the realisation of the highest.

Have an inward experience and a new you will emerge.

Kundalini opens the doors of perception to vast realms of Consciousness. Your meditation may include visions, lights, colours, sounds, journeys to archetypal realms, and infinite expanses of utter stillness throbbing with an absolute fullness of being.

Tears of joy may stream down your face as love beyond measure courses through your body.
The Kundalini's gifts are incomparable. After receiving them, no one is ever the same.

With awakened Kundalini energy you can build a healthy body, develop a balanced mind, make contact with your infinity, your innate inner wisdom as well as open the door so that you can exceed your full potential. It gives you the vitality and health that is your birthright. It makes you radiant, peaceful and strong so that you can deal easier with challenges of life.

There are many methods of awakening your Kundalini energy and I was fortunate to learn and practise Sahaja Yoga Meditation founded by Shri Mataji Nirmala Devi, a simple meditation technique for awaking your innate kundalini power.
She said, "You cannot know the meaning of your life until you're connected to the power that created you".
Sahaja Yoga Meditation was founded by Shri Mataji Nirmala Devi in 1970, who spread the practice from her native India to England and America, and then across the world and practised by millions of people.
She believed that enlightenment is not something that should be paid for, and so Sahaja Yoga classes have always been offered free of charge to all participants.

Sahaja Yoga meditation focuses on a network of energy channels (chakras) within the body known as the Subtle System, which starts in the sacrum bone, (sacrum Latin for secret) at the base of the spine, and rises up through the fontanel bone which was soft when we were babies, (fontanel Latin for little fountain) situated at the crown of your head.

When a person's inner energy is activated and begins to travel through the Subtle System, according to Sahaja Yoga philosophy, you will actually feel it being released "in the form of a cool, or sometimes warm, breeze.
This process is all started by raising your Inner Kundalini Energy. Kundalini travels starting in the sacrum at the base of your spine, and the energy is raised through all the Energy Centres, (Chakras) opening, clearing and activating them. After the energy has combined in the final Energy Centre at the crown of the head, it is released through the area where the fontanelle at the crown of the head used to be.
This self-realisation is also known as Yoga, (Yoga in Sanskrit meaning union).
For thousands of years in India and other places, the practice of Yoga was performed without any physical movement, in silence trough breading and deep meditation for the purpose of raising innate kundalini energy to be passed through our energy centres (chakras) purifying them and cleansing them in the process and finally rising through crown of the top of the head to be united with the energy of the divine.

◆ ◆ ◆
The true meaning of Yoga
is the union with the Devine.
◆ ◆ ◆

Have an inward experience and a new you will emerge.

And the purpose was lost over the years and is now known in the West as a form of exercise and physical movement.

Sahaja Yoga meaning:
Sahaja meaning: in Sanskrit comes from two words:
Saha meaning 'with' and ja meaning 'Born'.
Yoga meaning; in Sanskrit ' union.'

When we practice (Sahaja Yoga) meditation, our innate Kundalini Energy that we are all born with is awakened to be united with the divine.
Travels from the secret place, pass through our energy centres and at the little fountain, it's united with the Devine.
When this happens, it is called self-realisation. The more you practice meditation, you achieve more profound and stronger connection with the divine.

In a 2012 University of Sydney study, people who regularly practised Sahaja Yoga–style meditation had higher mental health scores than those who didn't. Meditation has also been linked to other health benefits, including stress relief, an improved immune system, and delayed signs of ageing.

There was medical research done on the benefits of Sahaja Yoga meditation conducted by Katya Rubia, a Professor of Cognitive Neuroscience at the Kings College London.
Prof. Rubia introduces the research that has been done on the effects of Sahaja Yoga meditation on our brain, body, health and mental and physical diseases.
She explains that meditation is a process of stopping our thoughts, which leads to the state of thoughtless awareness or mental silence. This state has been

described in all cultures and mystics by different names such as Yoga, Zen, Tao, Gnosis, etc.

Prof. Rubia claims that meditation is beyond normal relaxation because the state of thoughtlessness does not only help you to relax your body, but most importantly your mind, and it also helps you to become more emotionally resilient.

Subjectively, this state of mental silence leads to feelings of inner peace, of deep relaxation, of enhanced alertness, joy and detachment. With meditation, you can control your state of mind, your thoughts and your emotions. Scientific research has shown that these subjective experiences during meditation are, in fact, underpinned by significant effects on the body and the brain that reflect health benefits. Thus, meditation relaxes the body more deeply than simple relaxation and therefore leads to stress relief. Besides, it also leads to better mental balance, better attention and emotional resilience. Prof. Rubia introduces scientific evidence that meditation reduces stress by activating the parasympathetic nervous system that restores bodily functions, that meditation has a measurable effect on the brain by activating attention systems and the limbic system which is important for emotions and that it leads to better physical and mental health.

Professor Rubia conducted another study on the Increased Grey Matter Associated with Long-Term Sahaja Yoga Meditation practice.
The study shows that long-term practise of Sahaja Yoga Meditation is associated with larger grey matter volume overall, and with regional enlargement in several right hemispheric cortical and subcortical brain regions that are associated with sustained attention, self-control, compassion and interoceptive perception. The increased

grey matter volume in this attention and self-control mediating regions suggests use-dependent enlargement with regular practise of meditation.

With awakened Kundalini energy you can build a healthy body, develop a balanced mind, make contact with your infinity, your innate inner wisdom as well as open the door so that you can exceed your full potential. It gives you the vitality and health that is your birthright. It makes you radiant, peaceful and strong so that you can deal easier with challenges of life.
Be mindful of your inner peace not only during the meditation with your eyes closed but also throughout the day by witnessing your real self in the present moment.

As you begin to experience the benefits of daily meditation, your awakened kundalini, and your real self, you will start to emanate radiance, peace, confidence, compassion and love. You will awaken the same in people around you, and collectively we will begin to express out limitless potential and make the world a better place.

Meditate, Visualise and Create your own reality, and the universe will simply reflect back to you.
– Amit Ray

CHAPTER 19 - POSITIVE HABITS

Make lasting changes by paying attention to the smallest decisions we make – and their cumulative effect on us. It's about the slow burn, not the big gesture. It's about a marathon, not a sprint. By accepting responsibility for our own liv es, we can change our habits and carve out a life that is more successful, fulfilling and happy.
Reprogramming your subconscious mind, removing detrimental habit and installing a new program and a new positive habit requires consistent daily practice over several days.
Scientific research has shown that it will take fewer days for some people and more days for others to install the new program and a new habit.
The 21 Day Habit Theory was first introduced by Maxwell Maltz, a plastic surgeon in the 1950s
His theory was that it requires a minimum of about 21 days for an old mental image to dissolve and a new one to jell." Word spread and soon, the quote was shortened to: "It takes 21 days to form a new habit" …a term which stuck, and it was quoted since the 50s by several high profile authors in the self-help industry.
Dangerous lesson: If enough people say something enough times, then everyone else starts to believe it. It makes sense why the "21 Days" Myth would spread. It's easy to understand. The time frame is short enough to be inspiring, but long enough to be believable. And who wouldn't like the idea of changing your life in just three weeks?

So, is the theory accurate, and should you believe it?

I can't tell you that after 21 days of working on a habit, it will become embedded in your daily routine without ever having to worry about it again.
As we are all different and there are many factors to consider, it may take 18 days for some people and over 180 days for others.
A study in the European Journal of Social Psychology conducted by Phillippa Lally, a health psychology researcher at University College London analysed the habits of 96 people over 12 weeks. On average, it said that a habit takes around two months to become an automatic behaviour – 66 days to be exact. And for some can take up to eight months.

Note; they analysed the habits of ONLY 96 people and concluded that it takes on average 66 days to become automatic behaviour.
And how long it takes a new habit to form can vary widely depending on the behaviour, the person, and the circumstances. In Lally's study, it took anywhere from 18 days to 254 days for people to form a new habit.

In other words, if you want to set your expectations appropriately, the truth is that it will probably take you anywhere from two months to eight months to build a new behaviour into your life — not 21 days.

Since the above research was published, several people in the self-help industry started to quote the 66 days habit installation time as being a fact. I think this could also be risky to follow if you wish to achieve extraordinary success and install new habits.
It would be more accurate to suggest that you should try and test it for yourself by practising a new habit for several consecutive days and see how long it takes for you as a unique individual. It might only take 14 days.

No one template fits all as a lot of self-help books suggest. You should try, test and practice new positive habit for several consecutive days until you feel that it has become automatic and was stored in your subconscious mind. Remember when you first started learning the alphabet or the times table, you practised every day consecutively until it became an automatic habit, and you didn't stop there; you continued to use both daily.

At the end of the day, how long it takes to form a particular habit doesn't matter that much. Whether it takes 14 days or 254 days, you have to put in the work either way.

The only way to get to Day 254 is to start with Day 1. So forget about the number and focus on doing the work.

Interestingly, the researchers also found that "missing one opportunity to perform the behaviour did not materially affect the habit formation process." In other words, it doesn't matter if you mess up now and then. Building better habits is not an all-or-nothing process.

During the process of installing the new habit (disregarding how many days it takes you), there are four stages before it becomes an automatic habit.
1. Stage of awareness, learning, growing and removal of old habit
2. Stage of Inspiration, feel it in your heart
3. Stage of implementation
4. Stage of integration, atomic habit

Stage one; probably the most challenging and requires the most considerable amount of will power during which you will feel some or a lot of resistance from your old habits. A strong reason 'why' you need to change the old harmful habit would help tremendously during this stage.

You need a strong and compelling why.
I had two powerful reasons when I decided to make a
radical change in my diet — two very strong why's.
When I decided to change my diet entirely and became
vegan, eating only clean, whole food, unprocessed
vegetables and fruits, it was very challenging during the
first two weeks.
My first strong why was the negative impact my old
eating habits could have on my health.
I remembered how my late father suffering from poor
health for more than 23 years since he was 50 years old.
He had several heart surgeries and was in and out of the
hospital, suffering from heart disease, diabetes, dementia
and finally cancer before he passed away six and a half
years ago.
I had consulted several of his doctors in Melbourne,
Australia, where he lived, and all confirmed that my
father's health began deteriorating because of his diet.
His was a typical carnivore were he'd eat meat and
animal products three times per day and little or no
vegetables and fruit.

I know how much my father had suffered, my mother as
his carer and the rest of the family. So I promised myself
that I would do everything I can to change my eating
habits so I don't have the same fate. What's the point of
living if I will suffer for 20 or 30 years and spend most
of my days in the hospital, I thought.
My second strong 'why' was the fact that I love animals
and wowed that I will never eat them again. Knowing
what I know about soul and consciousness, there was no
way I will contribute to murdering another sentient
being.
During the first two weeks, I had some resistance from
my old eating habits, being reminded of the smell, taste
and texture of the dairy cheese, meat, fish, and eggs that
I used to eat regularly.

I used to eat eggs every day for breakfast, usually, with cheese, and fist two weeks of changing my habit was a struggle. I didn't know what to eat, and I wasn't aware that I knew so little about food.

I realised that I needed to learn so much about the vegan diet, practice recipes; it was all bit overwhelming at first. Each time I had breakfast, oats with almond milk and fruit, I would think of eggs and feel that there is no way oats and fruit would be sufficient to keep me going until lunch. I would eat vegetable stir fry, beans and rice, falafel for lunch or dinner and think of meat, chicken, and burgers.

The voice in my head was so strong in the first few days that almost had eggs for breakfast on a couple of occasions. I am glad I persevered and kept the promise I made to myself. My family and friends would also constantly tell me that I am crazy and asking me; why don't you eat meat; what's wrong with you they'd ask? Where do you get your protein from? Do you have to wake up every morning at 5 am to milk the almonds? I was struggling on my own during this first stage and naysayers around me didn't help.

Stage two; I began to read and learn more about the health benefits of a plant-based diet and how animals are suffering especially in industrial farming all around the world, and this inspired me and moved me in my core to persist. I remember the first time I watched a documentary by Kip Andersen named 'What a Health'. I broke down in tears upon seeing all the suffering of the animals, their abuse and their living conditions. I felt a strong emotion in my heart and was inspired to make it a life long habit. I would record that you find a strong why and get inspired through learning about your new positive habit, with this strong emotion, it will be a lot easier to succeed.

Stage three; started to feel bit easier, I've learned a lot about a vegan diet, bought a number of vegan cookbooks, practised many recipes, made amazing vegan banana bread and chocolate fudge brownies few times, had people over for dinner serving only vegan food that I had prepared. I was actually excited and looking forward to practising a new vegan recipe, and required less and less will power each day to mention my new habit. The old negative voice in my head, thinking about cheese and meat became quieter as I kept learning and implementing new healthy eating habits. I started to notice that I wasn't lethargic after a meal any more, I had more energy, my performance at the gym improved, I was getting stronger, lifting heavier, had no muscular sourness, and recovered faster after the workout. Day 20 and my new habit was becoming more and more automatic, and I still needed to be aware and remind myself of all the benefits and why I was implementing this new habit.

Stage four; by day 30 it became second nature for me to eat a healthy plant-based diet and it was interesting to observe that my inner peace wasn't disturbed any more when naysayers around me asked me if I was crazy for being vegan or asked me to justify why I am not eating meat. I knew at this point that this habit had become automatic and has remained so for many years now.

Note; my wife started on the same day with the plant-based diet, and It was perhaps a lot easier for me to implement this new eating habit.
Here is a secret; in stage four, you will require no will power and the benefits and rewards of the new habit will be visible and become automatic. By having this new habit running as an autocratic program, you will now have access to 100% of your will power to start installing a new habit.

I would recommend if possible to have a support
network around you, people that have the same
objectives. Have a coach, mentor or a friend to help you
implement your new positive habits. You could also
form accountability groups. Support groups that you
meet every week and present how well you did and if
you find something challenging learn how to overcome
it discuss your new commitments that of course come
with time constraints.

Habits are the compound interest of self-improvement.
The same way that money multiplies through compound
interest, the effects of your habits increase as you repeat
them. They seem to make little difference on any given
day, and yet the impact they deliver over the months and
years can be enormous. It is only when looking back
two, five, or perhaps ten years later that the value of
good habits and the cost of bad ones becomes strikingly
apparent.
But when we repeat 1 per cent errors, day after day, by
replicating poor decisions, duplicating tiny mistakes,
and rationalising little excuses, our small choices
compound into toxic results. Mastery requires patience
and persistence.
People struggle to develop and maintain new habits
because they make their efforts unsustainable.
They work out like crazy for a few days (usually at the
beginning of the year), and never go back to the gym.
They try to meditate for one hour one day and don't give
it another try until a week later.
They try to build a £100 million empire fuelled by a
burst of inspiration on a random Sunday afternoon and
never go back to the idea again.

Develop a habit of consistently doing something
positive. It doesn't matter what it is, or how small it is.

It could be as simple as going for a walk or meditating
for 5 minutes every day.
It could be doing ten pushups or ten sit-ups and 2
minutes of stretching.
It could be reading two pages of a self-help book or
listening to an audiobook for 10 min every day.
It could be as simple as snacking on an apple a day
instead of a chocolate bar.

The power of consistency is profound and underrated. It
can help you overcome a lack of natural talent, and
allow you to focus on the process instead of the prize.
If you can learn to do something consistently, you'll tap
into a much higher superpower than the habit itself: the
belief that you're completely capable of changing your
behaviour.
Once you're capable of changing your behaviour, you'll
be capable of making massive changes because little
things are done repeatedly lead to significant changes in
our lives.

Consistency creates momentum;
Momentum is based on the idea that an object in motion
stays in motion.
It's why it's more effective to write 200 words every day
than it is to write 1000 words once a week.
This is why we're better off practising an instrument for
15 minutes every day than we are an hour once a week.
It is why its better to go for a 2 mile run every day than
6 miles run once a week.
This is why it is better to reduce 200 calories a day than
1000 calories on a Saturday.
When we're consistent with anything that we do, we
stay in motion. When we remain in motion, we gather
momentum, which in turn becomes an automatic habit in
no time.

Doing small positive, smilingly insignificant actions daily and consistently over some time creates immense success.

Consistency is about building little empowering habits and rituals that you partake in every single day that keep you focused on your highest priorities and goals.

Consistency-in-action is not purely about repetition. It's rather about evolution.

It is not about mindlessly repeating an action over and over again. It's about learning, growing and adapting your actions that can help lead to incremental improvements over an extended period.

Consistency-in-action is about gaining ever more significant insights and understandings about what it is you are doing, and subsequently making the necessary adjustments to these actions to help improve your results and performance over the long-haul. In other words, it's all about improving your effectiveness and efficiency at each step of your journey. Therefore consistency demands that you stay vigilant and focused on making incremental improvements and not just sticking with the status quo.

To be consistent means understanding that the most significant power lies in the present moment. Therefore consistency demands that you stay vigilant, mindful and present on the tasks and results each day.

Habits are effectively just daily goals and most people's "goals" sound something like this:

Even though I haven't worked out in years, I'm going to train six days a week for 90 minutes a day and become a bodybuilder or a fitness model.

Even though I eat fast food four times a day right now, I'm going to eliminate all processed foods and eat salad five times a day.

Even though my body is used to waking up at 9 a.m., I'm going to start waking up at 5 a.m. every single day starting tomorrow.
Even though I am on my phone 20 hours a week doing trivial things and watch trivial shows for 20 hours a week, I will read one book a week starting tomorrow.

When you think about them in this way, most people's approach to forming new habits is so blatantly absurd. If you were to take the habits listed above and compound them by only 1% each day, in one year, you would have improved each habit of roughly 37%.

Jim Rhone said it beautifully; "Success is nothing more than a few simple disciplines, practised every day." He also said; "Learning is the beginning of wealth. Learning is the beginning of health. Learning is the beginning of spirituality. Searching and learning are where the miracle processes all begins."

Daily habits of self-made billionaires anyone can adopt

I've met several billionaires during my business career, and two of them are personal friends, mentors and have taught me a lot over the years. Billionaires are basically just the same as you and I, but what sets them apart is that they have mastered the art of emotional fitness, self-belief, and they came to realise that the only limitations any of us have are the ones we place upon ourselves. All billionaires, including the ones I know personally have several habits that they've been practising daily and continuously for years.

You may notice that none of them requires dramatic life changes — a few tweaks here and there to your daily routine could result in huge gains.

Meditation: They meditate twice a day; Ray Dalio, the founder of Bridgewater Associates, said: "Meditation, more than anything in my life, was the biggest ingredient of whatever success I've had." Jack Dorsey, CEO of both Twitter and Square wakes up at 5 am to meditate every day. Oprah Winfrey has said sitting in meditation for 20 minutes; twice a day instils in her a sense of hope, contentment, and joy.

They wake up early: Wealthiest people in the world tend to wake up three hours before their work actually begins, often before 6 am to exercise, practise gratitude, meditate, read, study, contemplate, write in their journal.

Routines: They have positive daily routines. Routines and rituals and sets of habits that, when practised consistently, lead to profound, long-term results. Most billionaires routines start early in the day. They stick to their routine even when they dint feel like it.

Live below their means: Just because they have billions in the bank they choose not to indulge in overspending, and many of them choose to live frugally.

Avid readers: Billionaires never stop learning and improving. They all have an unquenched thirst for knowledge. Warren Buffett reportedly spends about 80% of his day reading. Bill Gates reads more than 50 books a year. When Elon Musk was asked how he learned to build rockets, he reportedly answered, "I read books. As Jim Rhone puts it;" Formal education will make you a living; self-education will make you a fortune."

Exercise: Highly successful people don't just push themselves in the office — they push themselves physically, outside of the office. Richard Branson credits exercise for giving him at least four additional hours of productivity each day. Science concurs: Working out can boost your memory, concentration, and mental sharpness.

They socialise with other successful people: Billionaires believe what Jim Rohn said, "You are the average of the five people you spend the most time with." They hang out with other successful people, and they learn from one another. They only hang out with people with similar positive mindsets and avoid negative conversations.

Discipline: Billionaires set extraordinarily high standards for themselves and the people around them. In sports, for example, you can't achieve great results if you don't have enough discipline to train regularly. The same applies to your life and career. Limit the distractions and temptations that hinder your progress. Show up. Be eager to grow your skills. Of course, billionaires are by no means super-humans.
Like the rest of us, they have days where they feel lazy and unmotivated. The difference, however, is that they're fully aware of it and don't allow themselves to slack off. They power through their struggles.

Everybody wants to be successful — however, not many are willing to do the work. Don't leave your achievements up to chance. Instead of waiting for success or wealth to fall in your lap, take actionable steps every single day to inch closer to the life full of profound love, happiness, fulfilment and infinite abundance in every area of your life.

The way to make the best and quickest positive impact on the world, which is also sustainable, is by making sure that you work on yourself daily and constantly. Do deep internal work through meditation and remove any impediments (pains, traumas) that are holding you back, from recognising how amazing you already are, who and what you truly are — and becoming aware that you already are the infinite love, infinite abundance and infinite possibilities. As you do this and heal from within, you create a positive ripple effect on everyone around you and help heal the planet, and help improve the world.

Imagine a world where millions of people commit for the next ninety days to work on themselves, starting today. They divert their entire energy, and focus on healing and unveiling the best version of themselves, and in the process, heal the world.

I hope that by now you have practised meditation, other positive rituals, and you have fun living the knowledge of this book, bringing the childlike sense of wonder and passion to what you discover on the pages is one of the best ways to grow into the person I know you're meant to be.

With the information provided in this book you can confidently fly as a beautiful butterfly that you are and ascend to the greatest highest of who you truly are.

Thank you for giving me the privilege of sharing this work with you.

I wish for you a life abundant with love, joy, peace, magic, relationship bliss, profound happiness, and fulfilment, and I hope that you do your part in paying it forward and help in creating a better world.

"Heaven on earth it's a feeling, state of mind, an inward experience."

Support resources:
www.eldinhasa.com

For information on interviews, coaching sessions, talks, workshops, seminars, retreats, podcast and meditations given by Eldin Hasa see

www.eldinhasa.com

Facebook Community Group: Eldin Hasa Love & Positivity
In this group, we celebrate love, good in all of us and all around us — reminding us that the human spirit is infinite, with unlimited possibility and capable of inspiring love, compassion, joy, happiness, fulfilment and positive change.
As a community, we are here to support one another, elevate, and encourage us to want to be the best version of ourselves. To create engaging, uplifting and inspirational content that breaks through all the barriers. Building a community of sharing and igniting a movement that motivates people to celebrate and share the good in all of them and all around them. The community where everyone is contributing and collaborating from a place of solidarity and equality, love, and compassion.

Social media: @eldinhasa
Instagram, Facebook, Twitter

Podcast: The Human Experience
Could be found on iTunes, Spotify, Soundcloud and all major podcast platforms.
linker.ee/eldinhasa
Spreading Love & Positivity

This paperback edition published 2019 by Eldin Hasa
Publishing Limited

Copyright © Eldin Hasa
The moral right of the author has been asserted

Eldin Hasa Publishing Limited. Paperback Edition.
The right of Eldin Hasa to be identified as the author of
this work has been asserted by him in accordance with
the Copyright, Designs and Patents Act 1988

All rights reserved.
You may not copy, distribute, transmit, reproduce or
otherwise make available this publication (or any part of
it) in any form, or by any means (including without
limitation electronic, digital, optical, mechanical,
photocopying, printing, recording or otherwise), without
the prior written permission of the publisher. Any person
who does any unauthorised act in relation to this
publication may be liable to criminal prosecution and
civil claims for damages.

Eldin Hasa Publishing Limited
Paperback Edition
Kemp House 160 City Road London, EC1V 2NX
eldinhasa.com

www.ingramcontent.com/pod-product-compliance
Lightning Source LLC
Chambersburg PA
CBHW061503050726
47593CB00002B/434